T0318246

The Quarrel Between Poetry and Philosophy

The Quarrel Between Poetry and Philosophy: Perspectives Across the Humanities is an interdisciplinary study of the abiding quarrel to which poet-philosopher Plato referred centuries ago in the *Republic*. The book presents eight chapters by four humanities scholars that historically contextualize and cross-interpret aspects of the quarrel in question. The authors share the view that although poets and philosophers continually quarrel, a harmonious union between the two groups is achievable in a manner promising application to a variety of contemporary cultural-political and aesthetic debates, all of which have implications for the current status of the humanities.

John Burns is Visiting Associate Professor of Spanish Studies at Bard College. He has published the book *Contemporary Hispanic Poets: Cultural Production in the Global, Digital Age* and numerous book chapters, including "Teaching Infrarrealistas: Using Lesser Known Contemporary Poets in the Undergraduate Classroom" in *Teaching Latin American Poetries*, and "From Manifesto to Manifestation: The Infrarrealista Movement as an Alternative Latin American Literary Community" in *Alternative Communities in Hispanic Literature and Culture*.

Matthew Caleb Flamm is Professor of Philosophy at Rockford University. A scholar of Classical American Philosophy, he has published journal and book-chapter essays on George Santayana, John Dewey, and Josiah Royce. He has co-edited and authored four book-anthologies, including *Under Any Sky: Contemporary Readings of George Santayana* (with Krzysztof Piotr Skowronski) and *American and European Values: Contemporary Philosophical Perspectives* (with John Lachs and Krzysztof Piotr Skowronski).

William Gahan, Chair of the English Department and Faculty Trustee at Rockford University, is a native of Madrid, Spain. He has published translations of Renaissance Spanish literature in *Garcilaso's Tunisian Poems: A Bilingual Edition*, with Richard Helgerson for *A Sonnet From Carthage*. Gahan has published articles and book chapters on early modern literature and Shakespearean drama.

Stephanie Quinn is Associate Professor of Classical Studies at Rockford University. She has presented on Hermann Broch and Vergil at the Rocky Mountain MLA, at the Chicago Classical Club, and in January 2020, at the Society of Classical Studies panel on "Imperial Virgil." In October 2018, she spoke on "Circe at the Center of Virgil's *Aeneid*" at the Illinois Classical Conference. Her 2000 book, *Why Vergil? A Collection of Interpretations*, continues to be used widely as a reference.

Routledge Focus on Literature

Nineteenth-Century Italian Women Writers and the Woman Question
The Case of Neera
Catherine Ramsey-Portolano

The Quarrel Between Poetry and Philosophy
Perspectives Across the Humanities
John Burns, Matthew Caleb Flamm, William Gahan, and Stephanie Quinn

The Quarrel Between Poetry and Philosophy

Perspectives Across the Humanities

John Burns, Matthew Caleb Flamm, William Gahan, and Stephanie Quinn

Routledge
Taylor & Francis Group

NEW YORK AND LONDON

First published 2021
by Routledge
605 Third Avenue, New York, NY 10017

and by Routledge
2 Park Square, Milton Park, Abingdon, Oxon, OX14 4RN

First issued in paperback 2022

Routledge is an imprint of the Taylor & Francis Group, an informa business

Library of Congress Cataloging-in-Publication Data
A catalog record for this book has been requested

ISBN: 978-0-367-86335-7 (hbk)
ISBN: 978-0-367-55244-2 (pbk)
ISBN: 978-1-003-01849-0 (ebk)

DOI: 10.4324/9781003018490

Typeset in Times New Roman
by Apex CoVantage, LLC

Contents

Permissions

Selections of *Ave Soul* and *Tromba de agosto* by Jorge Pimentel reprinted by permission of Magreb Producciones SAC.

Acknowledgments

The authors would like to acknowledge the following persons who aided in the production of this book. We are grateful to the faculty of Rockford University for hosting two events on campus in which we were able to share early developments of our work. We are also grateful to the organizers of the 71st annual Rocky Mountain Modern Language Association, particularly Joy Landeira. As part of the conference, which was held in Spokane, Washington, in October 2017, we conducted a panel on this topic which helped us to better focus our ideas. Many informal conversations with colleagues at Rockford University and Bard College helped to shape this book. Particularly, at Rockford University, all our work would have been impossible without the interlibrary loan support of the Howard Colman Library and especially Audrey Wilson. Stephanie shared thoughts and received advice and encouragement from Sharon M. Bartlett, Marilén Loyola, Don Martin, and Patricia Walters. Stephanie also is grateful to the book group of John Jahring, Kevin Harrington, and Eileen Soderstrom, and especially to our group's leader Sally Kitt Chappell. This group has actually read Vergil and Broch, and Sally commented extensively on both of Stephanie's chapters in this book. John extends special thanks to Nicole Caso, Lauren Curtis, Cole Heinowitz, Patricia López-Gay, and Melanie Nicholson at Bard College who were of great help in thinking about this project at various stages. Matt thanks his mentor-colleague, Professor David Dilworth, SUNY Stony Brook University, New York, for inspiration on multiple key insights. Bill thanks Professors Stephen Deng from Michigan State University and Professor Michael O'Connell (UCSB, Emeritus) for early advice and encouragement. Bill, Matt, and John owe significant gratitude to Stephanie for her consistent motivation at various stages of labor, bringing to the authors' collective attention myriad vital details of arrangement and thematic conception. Matt, Stephanie, and Bill are also grateful to John Burns for his guidance and leadership with the proposal and publication process.

Introduction

Book Subject and Its Authors

Is truth found or is it made? About 2,400 years ago Plato referenced what he called "an old quarrel between philosophy and poetry."[1] The quarrel has been understood by many interpreters to be about which discourse— philosophy or poetry—accesses truth, and which one lies. The political and moral urgency of such a quarrel in relation to our times is expressed succinctly in a piece on "Retirement Tips for the Trump Era" by Charles J. Sykes: "you might realize what is most important: whether you stood firm in the truth when it mattered most."[2] The trouble of course is determining precisely the nature and meaning of "standing firm in truth"; of determining, by way of the use of language, what matters most in relation to truth.[3]

Socrates (469–399 BCE) was put on trial in Athens, Greece in 399 BCE for the charges of worshipping false gods and corrupting the youth. Many commentators have persuasively shown how the charges against Socrates were red herrings. If the charge of impiety had a basis at all, it is most likely to have been in regard to extenuating associations of Socrates with persons held in suspicion for their own suspected impiety. In 415 for example Socrates's admirer Alcibiades had come into conflict with Athenian adversaries over his suspected sacrilege and been condemned to death.[4]

The youth-corruption charge was at bottom an allegation that Socrates was inspiring rebellion in young persons against parents and state authorities. If anyone could fit that charge it might be the rhetorical enemies of Socrates, the sophists (many of whom counted among the "youth," or certainly exerted influence upon them), who taught the rhetorical skills needed to function in the deep but narrow Athenian democracy, where the ability to persuade in the courts and assemblies was essential for all citizens. That those skills could be abused—to make the weaker argument seem stronger—is gainsaid, then and now.

Such fifth-century BCE disputes about the nature of truth took place in tumultuous times. The successful Greek military encounters with the mighty

Persians at the beginning of the century confirmed the Greek city-states' confidence in their various democracies, especially at Athens, in what gradually emerged as an Athenian empire over fellow Greeks. Strife among the city-states dominated the century for the next 60 years. The plague of 426 BCE destroyed about one-third of Athens's population, including its leader Pericles. Athens's Sicilian expedition in 415 was disastrous.[5] Athens's destruction of the Greek island Melos was brutal. An oligarchy was enacted briefly in 411. By 404, Athens's military power was utterly destroyed, along with its ambitions for empire. The city-states contended for domination for about the next century, until a singular general, Alexander the Great, ended their hegemonic goals by conquering them all in the late 300s BCE.

In this context, Socrates was tried and executed in 399 BCE. Throughout the fifth century, sophists were claiming that they could persuade people of the truth of two opposite arguments. The great tragedians were articulating major issues and disputes of the times through their works for the wide Athenian and Greek audience. The context for Plato's great work was set. One aspect of his work about the nature of truth is articulated in the *Republic* as the "quarrel between poetry and philosophy." Our project for this book takes up the quarrel in several settings over the next 2,000 and more years.

This book is an interdisciplinary inquiry into the manner in which different modes of expression impact the reception and perception of truth. The poets Plato famously invoked are those who prioritize *making* in their approach to truth, while characteristic *philosophers* prioritize discovering. A more conventional way of putting this would be to say that poetic types (including but by no means limited to those who compose poetry), are creators, while philosophic types (including but by no means limited to those who compose philosophy) are searchers.

What sets this book apart from past studies is its uniquely interdisciplinary character. This book advances the conversation by showcasing collaborating authors with expertise in four different humanities disciplines, disciplines that refract the historical development of the philosophy-poetry quarrel itself: Classics (Quinn), English (Gahan), Philosophy (Flamm), and Spanish (Burns). The collective aim of the authors is twofold: to provide an historical understanding of what is at stake in the quarrels between poets and philosophers, and a sense of the cultural and political consequences of taking certain positions on poetic and philosophic modes of discourse. Such positions have to do with no less than the relation of language to truth, meaning, and experience.

A necessary word about the term "interdisciplinary." The term is fashionable in academic practice and too often gets used without purpose or thought, as though it is a good in itself to simply lump together different contributors with different forms of expertise. This book is no such random, ill-thought case of "interdisciplinary" collaboration. The collaborators began the project several years before the book's production, initially through personal-conversational affinity—an advantage afforded by the small liberal arts institutional setting they share—which then grew into successive conference events, the great success of which suggested the present book project. In other words, the interdisciplinary collaboration here is, to use a popular concept, "organic," and the grouping is a chief source of this book's strength.

As the brief chapter outlines included in this short introduction illustrate, this collaborative study is not restricted only to the meaning of the historical quarrel as connected with the tradition of Plato, but ranges across disciplinary and historical territories. The result, if you will, is a polyphonic display, one exploring different intersections of philosophy and poetry so as to illustrate how they sometimes cease altogether to quarrel. This book testifies, by way of exploring the manner in which different modes of expression impact the reception and perception of truth, to the harmonic possibilities of poetry and philosophy. Indeed the reader of this book should come to see how the question posed at the beginning of this first section, the question whether truth is "found or made," is distorting of the true relation between philosophy and poetry and leads to the kinds of political-moral conflict indicative of our times in the Sykes quotation.

Past Scholarship and How It Connects With This Book

Seminal single-authored monograph books and essays have been written on the ancient quarrel between poets and philosophers. The interesting fact about these works is that they all emphasize different aspects of and come to widely varying conclusions about the meaning and consequences of Plato's expression of the quarrel. In order both to provide a useful introductory glimpse of the trajectory of the scholarship, and also to indicate the need for a truly collaborative, interdisciplinary volume on the subject such as is the aim of the present one, three authoritative studies will be briefly noted.[6]

The first, Stanley Rosen, a key source-author for this book's theme, concludes that "the quarrel cannot be resolved"[7] and that Plato's writings establish that the advantage each form of discourse has over the other indicates their mutual need: "Philosophy has the advantage over poetry of being able to explain what it understands by wisdom. But poetry has the advantage over philosophy in that part of wisdom, and indeed the regulative part, is poetic."[8] For this reason, Rosen argues, both poetry and philosophy are needed. Left alone each discourse is given to certain tendencies of excess: "Philosophy without poetry, exactly like poetry without philosophy, is immoderate or unmeasured."[9]

A second important authority Thomas Gould provides a very different perspective. Gould sees the quarrel as having large-scale historical consequences for the fate of religion and culture in the West.[10] He understands the quarrel in terms strongly favorable to poetry and harshly indicting of philosophy, and resoundingly singles out Plato as responsible for the insidious historical reign of philosophy over poetry.[11]

Finally, a more recent, trenchant study by Susan B. Levin agrees as much with Gould as to say that Plato decisively favors philosophy over poetry. Agreements however end there. Her case lays altogether different emphasis than either those of Rosen or Gould on the conceptual ground of Plato's philosophy-privileging perspective. Whereas Gould focuses on *pathos* as the difference-making/grounding concept, and Rosen sees *eros* or human desire as fundamental to understanding the quarrel,[12] Levin contends that Plato's intent in the *Republic* is to demonstrate that "philosophy is the preeminent *technē*," that is, that philosophy, contrary to poetry, is of more "benefit" to society both because it provides a coherent "subject matter" and promised "understanding" of the same.[13]

The striking feature of these studies and many others that could be mentioned is that despite the diverging and in some cases contradictory conclusions reached, they do not cancel each other out; there is no decisive interpretive "winner" on the question. Each study contains quite different points of departure, develops different conceptual points of emphasis, and comes to conclusions that, while in some respects amenable to the others, provides an independently legitimate interpretation. Indeed one could argue that, while these studies independently maintain their clear importance for the development of literature on the quarrel in question, they at the same time illustrate the disciplinary insularity of the ongoing discussion.[14] This is why there is a clear need for a truly interdisciplinary study of the present kind.

Chapter Outlines

The opening chapter, "Origins of the Quarrel" by Matthew Caleb Flamm, provides an account of and historicizes the quarrel as originating in the writings of Plato, the great critic of forms of poetry whose voice reverberates through Western history. Flamm recalls the meaning and origins of the quarrel in question in the works of Plato, indicates where his own outlook intersects with authoritative scholarly interpretations, and comes to the following conclusion: poetry and philosophy stand at opposite, by no means *necessarily opposed*, poles of language.

The second chapter, "Vergil and Broch in Worlds Upside Down: Living the Quarrel Between Poetry and Philosophy" by Stephanie Quinn, examines

Hermann Broch's novel *The Death of Virgil* which is based on the Roman poet Vergil's dying day. Quinn establishes the interpretive immediacy of Broch's perspective. Reviewing the historical periods in which both Broch and Vergil lived, when long-settled world structures and views were crumbling, she acknowledges the reactions of artists and citizens of those times to the tumult, the upside-down character of those histories; the shared understandings across millennia that momentous change was underway, not just of political regime but of world historical consequence; and the shared instinct of political actors and artists to look to their distant pasts to understand a torturous present towards a deeply uncertain future. Quinn considers how amid such confusion, some artists questioned, even despaired, of the ability of art to say true things when the truth itself was in turmoil. Some thinkers and artists, she observes, perceived these opposite and contradictory uses of Vergil, especially through his epic, the *Aeneid. The Death of Virgil* uses the ancient biographical tradition of Vergil's wish that the *Aeneid* be destroyed after his death to develop a (more than) Joycian rumination on the power of art for good or ill and its ability to say true things in history. Quinn helps readers appreciate how Vergil and Broch, across 2,000 years, were grappling with the quarrel between poetry and philosophy.

Chapter 3, "Lessons, Lies, and Legacies: The Place of Poetry in Thomas More's *Utopia* and Philip Sidney's *Defense of Poesy*" by William Gahan, shows that many early modern English texts conformed to the two modes of expression stipulated previously. That is, poetic "making" versus philosophical "discovering" of truth. Thomas More and Sir Philip Sidney, with ambiguity and irony, championed the truth-making character of poetry (understood as all imaginative writing). More's *Utopia* explores the value and necessity of imaginative thinking in the face of conflicting biases in politics and life, and the limits of language. With equally subtle irony, Sidney's *Defense of Poesy* reinterprets Plato and affirms the salutary nature of poetry's potential to instruct, delight, and create legacies. In saying that poetry does not lie because it "nothing affirms," Sidney celebrates the human ability to create "new natures," all the while implying the need for comfort with the indeterminacy of language in any honest approach to truth.

Chapter 4, "La Malinche and the Noble Lie" by John Burns, explores the representation of La Malinche, a central figure in the Spanish conquest of Mexico to exemplify some of the real-world implications of the concepts that Plato introduced in the *Republic*. She was known in different cultural settings by different names: Malinalli or Malintzin in her native tongue, doña Marina for the Spanish, La Malinche in subsequent Mexican history. Burns considers how she has been represented in the chronicles of the conquest and in more contemporary literary imaginings in such a great variety of ways that they are difficult to reconcile with a single historical personage.

The multiple projections of meaning onto the relative blank screen La Malinche's biography develop in ways that elucidate Plato's considerations of the relationship between poetry and the ideal state, as well as the nature of myth making.

In Chapter 5, "Making and Discovering in Shakespeare's Sonnets,"[15] William Gahan discusses the sonnets in light of Plato's ousting of the poets from the *Republic* for telling lies. The sequence performs what Sidney and More suggest that poetry can achieve: although language is limited, it is all we have, and only imaginative creation can conceive of a permanent ideal (a "fixed mark"). However, the sequence does not attempt to ennoble the reader, as Sidney and More suggest for poetry. Shakespeare conjures Platonic ideals poetically, but he upends every attempt to follow them through absolutely, and the sequence enacts a process of continual "making," "discovering," and failing. That the ideals proposed in the sonnets fail in the face of human and linguistic limitations shows that they were always poetically-conceived ideals—not attainable truths—and this suggests that Plato's ideas as conceived in the *Republic* partake of poetic creation too. Rather than ennoble, the sonnets effectuate a rhetorical display of skill that may outlast all others, conferring a legacy on the memory of the poet and his love.

In the sixth chapter, "Vergil, Broch, and a "Place" for Art: Answering the Quarrel," Stephanie Quinn extends the analysis of her previous chapter, showing how the methods of Vergil and Broch can be used to examine the quarrel. Quinn shows how competing, contradictory realities challenged ancient and modern contemporaries and artists with the philosophical problem of telling the truth. Vergil's structure and Broch's language reproduce the historical, philosophical, and literary problematic. Vergil answers the quarrel, Quinn contends, through yet another Platonic device, the "place" or *chôra* of the late dialogue, *The Timaeus*. She helps readers appreciate how Broch's text names the problem of an artistic place for truth.

In Chapter 7, "Jorge Pimentel: Obfuscation for Clarity's Sake," John Burns extends the examination of the ancient quarrel to include a consideration of twentieth-century experimental poetry, specifically, the work of Jorge Pimentel, a member of Hora Zero, a group of poets in Peru who began publishing their work in the early 1970s. Pimentel's work within the group could be read as a microcosm for twentieth-century poetry in general: by turns open and accessible and then hermetic and markedly difficult. In the movement between clarity and difficulty, Pimentel not only embodies many of contemporary debates around lyric poetry but is in itself a contemporary variation on the ancient quarrel between poetry and philosophy. Burns's chapter carefully "translates" between disciplines in the humanities, from Plato into Pimentel, that is to say, from classical philosophy into radically experimental contemporary poetry, along the general axis of mistrust about language.

The final book chapter, "Turning With Heidegger Towards Poetry" by Matthew Caleb Flamm, examines key aspects of the work of twentieth-century philosopher Martin Heidegger (1889–1976) which provides a counter to the poetry-deriding history bequeathed from Plato. When quoting German poet Friedrich Hölderlin's "Patmos," Heidegger expresses directly (appropriately, *in* poetry) the solution to the conflict Plato long ago effectively established: "We may know something about the relations between philosophy and poetry, but we know nothing of the dialogue between poet and thinker, who 'dwell near to one another on mountains farthest apart.'"[16] Following Plato's insistence that poetry-lovers "say in prose" how poetry is not only "pleasurable" but also "beneficial," Heidegger's (Hölderlin's) point is that Plato and like-minded critics of poetry are blind to the "near-*dwelling*" of poets and philosophers. It is the out-of-scale ("mountainous") relation of the interpretive positions occupied, respectively, by philosopher and poet that necessitates both their estrangement and mysterious interconnectedness.

Final Words: How This Study Connects With Culture, History, and Politics

These collaborating perspectives illustrate the resilience of the interplay between what Charles L. Griswold calls the "making" power of poetry and the "discovering" power of philosophy.[17] As this interdisciplinary project aims to show, "making" and "discovering" are co-conspiring aspects of the same interpretive endeavor. Imaginative thinking lends meaning and shape to memory and experience.

The studies in this volume show that life's experiences are made meaningful through imaginative writing and thinking (narrative, rhetoric, and poetry), and this meaning-making has foundational consequences to disciplinary study in addition to many other facets of experience and politics, including the formation of personal, national, and cultural identities.

This book as a whole illustrates how the ancient quarrel between poetry and philosophy can serve as a platform for investigating any number of opposite and seemingly warring perspectives, both perennial and current: facts, evidence, reason, science, mathematics, data, research, logical argument on the one hand; and on the other, common sense, religious truth, fake news, subtlety, spirituality, the ineffable. In other words, all these approaches, which seem incompatible intellectually and are sometimes political and social enemies, yet all aim for, are devoted to the search for the truth. Indeed one could say with some justice that our current so-called crisis of the humanities and the liberal arts and sciences is coterminous with crises in politics and public discourse. The health of the humanities has consequences in public life. This volume aims not to argue that point, but to demonstrate it.

We hope our varied excursions into this topic resonate across disciplines and especially across perspectives. It is our culture's essential inheritance to fight among ourselves about these matters. The ways we will continue to conduct these arguments in the twenty-first century—in the academy and in the public square—can affect nothing less than the ability of freely associating people of many and great differences to sustain a well-functioning and fair society. Times are no more urgent for the ancient and ongoing quarrels between poets and philosophers to be assessed by four different, yet intersecting, disciplinary perspectives within the humanities.

Notes

1. "There is an old quarrel between philosophy and poetry" (*Republic*, 607b5–6). Estimated date of text, 380 BCE. All *Republic* citations C.D.C. Reeve translation (Hackett Publishing Company, 2004).
2. *NYT* January 7, 2019, page SR2. Similarly, the new publisher of the *New York Times*, A.G. Sulzberger, in a January 5 email letter to subscribers noted a rise in "misinformation" and concluded among other things that "truth matters."
3. A matter all the more problematic living as we do in a time of unprecedented manipulation of modes of mass communication: manipulations of information and data systems that have involved the use of information and technology to alter major election outcomes and to sway and mold public perceptions of truth.
4. Forcing him to flee Athens for a time to advise Sparta in the long and momentous Peloponnesian war (431–404).
5. Connected with the aforementioned suspicion of impiety of Alcibiades: on the eve of this expedition statue heads of the god Hermes were mutilated throughout Athens. Alcibiades, who was then empowered to lead the Sicily campaign on behalf of Athens, was fingered, reportedly by false witnesses, and never again recovered his full reputation among Athenian authorities.
6. The present authors found it noteworthy that among extant studies only one is comparably collaborative and interdisciplinary to the present volume: the Volume 1, number 2 2015 edition of the *Odradek* journal, which contains nine different scholarly essays on the theme. This book differs significantly from that collection in a few key respects: first, the authors here came together by mutual sympathy and understanding, the renowned authorities in that edition of *Odradek* were solicited by residing editors. Second, outside of Plato, a necessary figure looming in any study on the quarrel in question, none of the other figures covered are duplicated. Third, the contributions to the *Odradek* collection—wonderful in themselves and indeed consulted for the present study—do not interconnect and indeed could easily have been published as stand-alone pieces in another authoritative journal without the need for the overall thematic framing.
7. Stanley Rosen. *The Quarrel Between Philosophy and Poetry.* Routledge, 1988: 26.

8. Rosen, 13.
9. Rosen, 26.
10. "The quarrel Socrates and Plato picked with the tragedians [poets] was theological in the first instance." Thomas Gould. *The Ancient Quarrel Between Poetry and Philosophy.* Princeton University Press, 1990: 225.
11. Strongly contrary to Rosen's view that Plato's writings establish no definitive preference for poetry or philosophy, Gould sees Plato's writings "at odds with the poetic tradition in general and tragedy in particular" (Gould, 7).
12. "[T]he quarrel between philosophy and poetry [as understood in relation to Plato's *Republic*] has evolved from one that is political in the conventional or usual sense into a more fundamental quarrel between two ways of responding to human desire, or, to give desire its official Platonic name, Eros" (14).
13. Susan B. Levin. *The Ancient Quarrel between Philosophy and Poetry Revisited: Plato and the Greek Literary Tradition.* Oxford University Press, 2001: 135; 142. This claim of Levin's directly intersects with the important challenge Socrates raises to poetry-lovers at the end of the *Republic* in which he suggests they must be able to say "in prose" what makes poetry both pleasurable and "beneficial" (something that he has argued can be said of philosophy). Levin gathers together various suggestions from diverse works of Plato—including especially the *Cratylus* and *Phaedrus*—to argue against those (such as Gould) who see Plato as a sheer foil for literature/poetry; those in particular who use Plato's example to mount a case for poetry *against* philosophy.
14. One case in point, Levin, a scholar of philosophy, engages in her study the Classics scholar Gould extensively but does not cite or even acknowledge fellow philosophy scholar Rosen.
15. I use "making" as "discovering" in the sense Griswold does. See the "Final Words" section of this introductory chapter.
16. Heidegger, Martin. "Postscript to 'What is Metaphysics.'" *Existence and Being. A Gateway Edition.* Henry Regnery Co. Chicago, 1949: 360..
17. As the chapters explore in what follows, these characterizations follow the etymological-historical meaning of these concepts.

1 Origins of the Quarrel

Matthew Caleb Flamm

At the end of Plato's *Republic* Socrates expresses a concern connected with what he calls an "old quarrel between philosophy and poetry."[1] The concern is whether the ideal state he has envisioned might be seen by certain persons as "harsh" and "boorish."[2] The persons Plato-Socrates seems to have had in mind were the truth-sanctioners of their contemporary Athens, those who apparently esteemed Homer as the supreme poet, indispensable towards the "arrangement of one's whole life."[3] Such persons, from his point of view, privilege poetry without the needed support of philosophy. Socrates's concern is warranted given that in his greater text he has elevated the philosopher to ruler-status and has argued that a correct state education would banish the sort of poetry loved (apparently too much) by appointed truth-sanctioners, which is merely *imitative*, "incapable of teaching virtue,"[4] and at a "third remove from truth."[5]

Socrates's case against poetry in his ideal state leaves a door open. As a kind of final offer of fair play Socrates tells Glaucon that poetry-defenders should be invited to "argue without meter [i.e., to argue in prose rather than poetry] on her behalf," to prove to poetry's doubters:

> that she gives not only pleasure but also benefit both to constitutions and to human life. Indeed, we will listen to them graciously, since we would certainly profit if poetry were shown to be not only pleasant but also beneficial.
>
> (607d)

Socrates cannot for a moment believe such a defense of poetry can be made. He has already argued persuasively that poetry is ill-suited for an ideal education because its storytelling is "neither true nor beneficial" (386c). In the *Republic*, Book III 386a–398, Plato provides his most explicit call for the censorship of most forms of poetry in association with education of the young. He identifies certain aspects of poetry that provide "what our young people need" (389d), then calls for a banishment of all but the "simplest" and "purest" poetry. The mercilessly demoted admissible poet is one who is a "pure imitator of the good person" (397d), whose tone aspires simply to the courageous, honorable soldier:

> just leave me that harmony that would appropriately imitate the vocal sounds and tones of a courageous person engaged in battle or in other work that he is forced to do, and who—even when he fails and faces wounds or death or some other misfortune—always grapples with what chances to occur, in a disciplined and resolute way.
>
> (399b)

At one point he narrows all poetry and storytelling down to two "styles," the first permissible one "involves little variation" in an "appropriate harmony and rhythm," the second censurable style involves "every harmony and every rhythm" and is "multifarious in the forms of its variations" (397c). In sum, only the most benign, saccharine, stale, conventional, and inevitably *unpoetic* of poetry remains admissible. This fulfills Socrates's conception of ensuring a "proper" education, where the only beneficial type of poetic storytelling is that of a "pure imitator of the good person" (397d), and where only the simplest kind of tone/presentation/meter is acceptable, and where the poet does "not chase after complexity or multifariousness in the basic elements" (399e). Socrates's proposal to Glaucon at the end of the *Republic* is in other words a fool's offer. No poet worthy of the name visiting Plato's State would be able to prove his work *beneficial* as well as pleasant.

And Plato's call was answered. Whether Plato's perspective is correct that poetry and philosophy were already long quarreling by the fourth century BCE[6] it is at least clear that, as the authors of this book agree, this quarrel resounded throughout the post-Platonic West and is as much with us today as ever.

Of course the historical influence of this lone aspect of Plato's diverse writings is complex. Thomas Gould argues that the *Socratism* introduced by Plato's writings changed the course of Western religion and morality.[7] Gould argues that Plato's philosophy ("Socratism") forced a shift from reliance on a pre-Socratic ideal of *pathos* wherein humans can be *expected to suffer* for their inability to attain to divine expectation, to reliance on a post-Socratic ideal wherein even divine intervention is understood to conform to human conceptions of justice and morality. Put another way, Gould argues that Plato's thinking, in order to establish the righteous authority of human reason by way of dialectical argumentation, forced God into conformity with reason.[8]

The grandiosity of Gould's thesis may have deficiencies,[9] but its resonance with other major interpretations makes it useful.[10] It is provocative for the theme of this book that poetic vision became in the West, by way of Socratic tradition, subordinated to human-legislating reason.

Gould argues that Socratism rejected the "spectacle of pathos," a phenomenon vividly displayed in the figure of Oedipus, whose suffering "makes one shudder and want to turn away, even as it makes one yearn to look . . . and try to understand."[11] It is this latter, "try to understand" aspect of Sophoclean-*poetic* pathos that the *Republic*-Plato was banishing; the danger of this sort of poetry, its tendency to promote "undesirable" passions instead of logical understanding, is found in its failure to provide true knowledge. Whatever may be accomplished by Sophoclean-poetic pathos, it could not in Plato's understanding deliver true knowledge.

A main contention of this chapter is that the undesirable passions targeted by Plato's assault on poetry evolved in the West into a general assault on darkness, into a pathological adherence[12] to the divine light of rational understanding as a means of escaping darker territories of human understanding and endeavor. Besides gleaning this view from Gould, it has a wide currency in critics inspired by Nietzsche's articulation of the "Problem of Socrates" according to which Socrates/Plato made a "tyrant out of reason" and sought to "counter the dark desires by producing a permanent *daylight* of reason."[13] This pathology, entailing as it does a nuanced bias against poetic expression, has inspired Western poets and kindred artists into a posture of rebellion, into a role symbolized beautifully in Thomas Hardy's "aged thrush," whose "voice arose" one death-surrounded winter evening "in a full-hearted evensong of joy illimited . . . thus to fling his soul upon the growing gloom."[14]

It is important to acknowledge that poetry *before* Plato's writings was already starting to encounter the challenge prophesied in the *Republic*. Gould for example identifies earlier echo-signs of the rift within the corpus of Homer. Whereas Homer's *Iliad* "gives us a universe in which the most splendid men and women can expect to experience terrible suffering at the hands of the gods," the "poet of the *Odyssey*, by contrast, insists that by and large justice is done and men who deserve happiness will experience it eventually."[15] The shift to a morally-elect conception of the human suffering occurred within the corpus of Homer; that it occurred in echo-fashion in Plato's thinking underscores that the revolt against a particular style of poetry involved, as Gould articulates, an inverted relation between humans and the divine.

Of course poetry did not go away after Plato, rather, ever after it was forced to answer for its perceived inability to yield correct understanding, a mantle that Western philosophy would take up on poetry's behalf for centuries to come. A simmering example is the advent, beginning around the eleventh century in the Medieval West, of so-called vernacular poetry initiated by the troubadours of southern France and northern Italy.[16] Around 1304, in a cultural context entirely removed from Plato's, Dante effectively answered the call to defend poetry to its doubters when he wrote *De Vulgari Eloquentia*, "On Eloquence in the Vernacular."[17] Dante's career attests that the great Western poets were forced to grapple with appointed power-brokers of language. Dante's fourteenth-century Italian context had put the poet into the position prophesied by Plato: he felt it necessary to show in *De Vulgari Eloquentia* (in the clerically-sanctioned language),[18] that poetry was both beneficial and useful.

But Plato's corpus is diverse and there is tremendous risk of misrepresentation summarizing his understanding of poetry via the *Republic* alone.[19] To see this more clearly, consider the parallel interpretation of the origins of the philosophy-poetry rift from Stanley Rosen. In contrast to the "suppression of pathos" thesis of Gould, Rosen emphasizes the suppression of *eros*, or erotic love: "[Plato's] just city may be described as an attempt to suppress Eros, both of body and psyche."[20] Famously, Plato relegates sexual relations in his Ideal State to a role aiding the attempt to "inculcate self-mastery in young people" (*Republic* 390b) which entails regulatory leadership from philosopher-rulers capable of "ascertaining the periods of good fertility and of infertility for [the] species" (546b). In Book V Plato/Socrates insists that all spouses and children be held in common, a practice ensured by designating time-appropriate sex festivals in which the fittest guardians are matched with spouses for the duration of copulation to produce the fittest children (who are then sent off to "fit" caregivers, not the biological parents). He goes so far as to say that children born of guardians outside of designated sex festivals be killed (461c).[21]

Rosen emphasizes the nuances in Plato's writings on this point by bringing this *Republic*'s regulatory imperative to suppress eros into connection with the treatment of eros in the *Symposium*, which, in its association of love with madness indicates the seeming paradoxical "erotic necessity" of philosophy itself.[22] Since philosophy itself is a form of love (love of wisdom), there is a move in Plato's project to reconcile the public regulation of eros—necessary so as to correctly govern unenlightened non-philosophers—with the private flourishing of philosophic activity among enlightened ruler-philosophers. In the *Symposium* Plato supplements the regulatory erotic social program of the *Republic*, which pivots on a censorship of "impure" poetry, with a philosophic "love of the beautiful in itself, [which] in the *Symposium* is the peak of the transition from love of things to love of Ideas."[23] In this way for Plato, Rosen concludes, "philosophy [becomes] not simply the sum of mathematics and poetry, but the completion of each."[24]

And yet the differences between Plato's outlook and the Christian understanding which developed from it indicate that his settling of the quarrel in question here would be ever vulnerable to the turbulence of historical change. It is striking for example to observe that the public regulation of sexuality envisioned by Plato would appear to post-Platonic Christians on the one hand objectionable in its permissive allowance of sexual non-exclusivity, yet on the other laudable in its suppression of wanton, hedonistic, non-procreative sex. In parallel fashion, as one sees in Gould's analysis, the Socratic rejection of dark poetic pathos entails what to a Christian outlook would be a double commitment: on the one hand to the denial of ambiguous symbolism (dangerous poetry that "corrupts"), and on the other to the self-sacrificing embrace of theocratically-authorized forms of symbolic worship. In other words, whether one sees the problem from Gould's or Rosen's point of view, something deeply divided lies at the heart of the Christianized West. Both interpretations enable one to appreciate how Platonism/Socratism introduced into the Western spiritual climate a conflicted attitude towards poetic expression that contorted the direction of religion and its cultural influences.

Yet still, as suggested, consideration of Plato's larger corpus might challenge the contention that this conflict took such a hold on the ensuing Western psyche. Is the legacy of Plato one of *mis*-appropriation? Probably not.

Silke-Maria Weineck shows for example how Plato's *Phaedrus*, a dialogue one scholar calls the "closest of any dialogue to having a structure that is a passkey for every other dialogue,"[25] Socrates "explicitly links poetry to philosophy."[26] He does so however in a manner that creatively reinstates the concluding proposal of the *Republic* in which Socrates invites poets to argue in prose on behalf of poetry. As seen in the *Republic* Socrates offered this invitation with the expectation of its failure: he knows such a poetry defense could never be convincing in a philosophy-privileging context in which the supreme task is education and rearing of the young towards the appropriate placement of citizens. In such a context poets speaking about the "benefits" of poetry to its doubters have loser's odds.

By comparison, in the conversational context of the *Phaedrus*, a kindred-dialogue to *Symposium* about the nature of love, Socrates's discourse suggests the marriage of poetry and philosophy. The marriage is achieved through a process of *recantation* or argumentative reversal (a method not unlike the dialectical method of Hegel centuries later). Socrates provides three speeches that rhetorically progress towards truth by way of a controlled poetic madness, culminating in an uncanny clarity of understanding befitting the sublime theme of love. Each previous speech is surpassed and refuted, achieving a consummatory understanding that constitutes a reconciliation of the otherwise oppositional tendencies of poetry and philosophy.

But there is a catch, one nudging the anti-poetry stance of the *Republic* yet further over the edge. Weineck writes that: "Socrates never says [in the *Phaedrus*] that poetry might be philosophical, only that poets who can critique their own work might be philosophers."[27] It will take (in her view) centuries for a notion of truly "philosophical poetry" such as is found in the work of Friedrich Hölderlin[28] to emerge.

A meaningful distinction between philosophy and poetry is begged. Stanley Rosen and Charles Griswold convey the difference between the concepts in terms of *discovering* (philosophy) versus *making* (poetry). Probably today when one hears "poetry," the idea of lyric, form, and free verse comes to mind. Truer to its Greek roots[29] poetry in the sense that is important here is any form of communicative expression (speech or writing) whose chief aim is *to make*. More explicitly, Plato maintained that the effort of the poet is *to make appearances*.

To the contemporary ear these meanings, etymologically accurate as they are, tend to encourage a prevalent derogatory perception of poetry; the perception that poetry hovers on the surface of things in the sense of triviality and irrelevance. But when one probes more deeply into the meaning of poetry, "not," as George Santayana indicates, "in the formal sense of giving a minimum of what may be called by that name," one is invited to see a connection between poetry and spirituality. When it achieves its aspirations poetry is "a momentary harmony in the soul amid stagnation or conflict—a glimpse of the divine and an incitation to a religious life":

> Religion is poetry become the guide of life, poetry substituted for science or supervening upon it as an approach to the highest reality. Poetry is religion allowed to drift, left without points of application in conduct and without an expression in worship and dogma; it is religion without practical efficacy and *without metaphysical illusion*.[30]

Enhanced as this insight is by the fact that it is delivered by an accomplished philosophical poet and interpreter of Christian tradition,[31] it stands on its own as inviting one to consider the true meaning of the making-power of poetry: poetry "makes appearances" not in the trivial sense of playing with words and meanings but in a vital sense potentially lending a spiritual meaning to an otherwise empty, overwhelming existence.

Here is where, historically speaking, philosophy has asserted its authority. Philosophy, in its historical meaning, "discovers," "finds." As Griswold writes:

> Philosophers . . . are presented [first by Plato, later certified in Modern philosophy in Cartesian and Kantian traditions] as committed to the

pursuit of truth that is already 'out there,' independently of the mind and the world of becoming. Their effort has to do with discovery rather than making."[32]

This conception of philosophy is attributed by deconstructionist interpreters inspired by (among others) Heidegger to the modern/pre-modern commitment to a "metaphysics of presence," a metaphysics that privileges what is present over what is absent. The "out there" reached for by Western philosophers in the wake of Plato is based on a subject-object relation that presumes reality and truth to be a "given" element of experience, discreetly present to an observing, independent consciousness. Such a standpoint could not be further from that of the poet for whom presence is not a subject-object relation, for whom, as T.S. Eliot articulates, there is neither an objective external reality, nor a discreet subjectivity, but instead a yet-undistinguished reality poetically probed in order to attain an "objective correlative." The "objective correlative" that Eliot identifies as the goal of poetic activity has its standard in a present "particular emotion."[33] For the poet, as opposed to the philosopher, presence is not a *metaphysical* presumption about the subject-object nature of reality; it is in fact a standpoint prior to any metaphysically differentiating interpretation—it is, as Santayana expresses in the previous excerpt, "religion without metaphysical illusion." Indeed when poetry achieves its aim, due to its suspension of metaphysical assumptions, it is an opening *into* reality exactly at the margins of interpretation.

And it is precisely because of the legacy of Plato's quarrel that this conception of poetry has eluded Western philosophers and has forced them only in relatively recent history to devise various creative (if fraught with other issues) strategies of poetry-recovering. A well-known reference point is the work of many key postmodern philosophers,[34] among them Heidegger, John Dewey, and Ludwig Wittgenstein, the beautifully selected triumvirate of Richard Rorty's 1979 manifesto *Philosophy and the Mirror of Nature*. Postmodern philosophers in this vein[35] have challenged the Western philosophic metaphysics of presence, and the correspondence theory of truth which is its ground and sanction.[36]

In their *finding* mode of searching, traditional Western philosophers have insisted upon interpretive closure. *Making* poets have meantime operated in a mode of interpretively open suspension. The historical privileging of philosophic-finding modes of interpretation is seen in its cultural results, not least of which is the rise and reign of scientific expertise in modern times. The finding-mode of interpretation, preeminently defined by the contemporary sciences, is the anointed authority in contemporary life, regarding which everywhere one encounters appeals to closure. "We *now* know that," "studies have *shown*," "it can no longer be disputed that," and all manner of such appeals have at their heart the aim to close down inquiry. Further inquiry, indeed, would be pretentious, purporting to know more than "*is*" known (an inquiry-closed domain).

The pretense that centuries ago Socrates objected to in poets[37] had to do with their efforts at truth-making. Where poetry surpasses its office of truth-making (and perhaps purports to have some role in truth-discovering), it serves what Plato called "the childish passion that the masses have [for] such poetry [as is] not to be taken seriously, as a serious undertaking that grasps truth" (*Republic* 608a). When it comes to truth-getting, only a "serious undertaking" should be tolerated culturally speaking; the seriousness of such an endeavor is established by *discovery*, not making. And so, because discovery-seeking philosophers and making-poets alike aim at truth, it is their *interpretive relation to* truth for Plato that makes for grasping their "proper" and "improper" roles.

It begs one to consider, since Plato restricts himself to the misapplication of poetry, whether there would not be an equal and opposite misapplication of philosophy? Is it in those instances where philosophers surpass their office of truth-discovering and purport to have a role in truth-making? This delicate consideration is taken up in the chapters to follow. Just here, returning to the relation between human and divine, and the privileging of philosophy over poetry which amounts to privileging the human over the divine, the historical-cultural impact on poetry itself needs to be expressed. Stated directly, I conclude here with the following contention: due to its historically subordinate status to philosophy, poetry in the West has taken up the mantle of darkness.

Given the rise and reign of science, technology, medicine, and quantitative reasoning in modern times it should not surprise to find commentators characterizing the ancient quarrel in terms favorable to poetry; revealingly, reflecting the historical legacy just discussed, those terms always take the form of apologetics. Raymond Barfield writes, for example: "the poet is always after the mystery that god who is unknown can be revealed only as the one who is unknown . . . philosophy returns again and again to poetry because philosophy needs the gods."[38] Philosophy continually "returns" from its place of privilege, culturally speaking. The precise thing traditional Western philosophy "needs" from the gods is what it falls short of providing itself in all of the brilliant light of its discoveries: the leftover darkness, the "ever not quite" spoken of by American philosopher William James, "the word '*and*' [that] trails along after every sentence."[39]

When, as Gould argues, Socrates ran around Athens "insisting that his fellow citizens reject as dangerously false any story that moves men with depictions of divine injustice,"[40] make no mistake, this was a concern for the consequences of the influence of darkness. The fault of (most forms of) poetry for Plato, as Gould argues, is its dangerous pathos; its ability to induce awareness of the irremediable, of that about which nothing is to be done. It has been a long-term strategy in the cultural West to identify the "dangerous" elements in creative expression, indicate the sense in which if they are let to influence, especially, vulnerable developing minds, the latter will be harmed. This establishes the inevitability that the state as a whole is at risk and opens a powerful means of inducing large numbers of people to support censuring cultural policies, and of enforcing acceptance of narrow, shallow, dark-suppressing, light-propagating forms of expression.

Contrasted with the decisive authoritativeness of philosophy, poetry is elliptical, ambiguous, suspended in the *ever not quite*.[41] Attempting to explain the elliptical office of poetry, William S. Allen writes:

> The poet's experience is initially that of the ability of names to bring things into being; this is his craft, but then he discovers that there is one thing he cannot name and in that moment it disappears . . . the poet learns [in this experience] a more searching lesson than that of his ability to name things to their being, something that turns him away from his earlier craft.[42]

This opening into darkness is from the standpoint of the light-obsessed philosopher nothing but a menace, an obstacle to legitimate understanding.

In his study *Three Philosophical Poets* (Lucretius, Dante, and Goethe), Santayana wrote: "even if we grant that the philosopher, in his best moments, is a poet, we may suspect that the poet has his worst moments when he tries to be a philosopher, or rather, when he succeeds in being one."[43] By placing this interesting sentiment in connection with Weineck's thesis that Plato refuses the opportunity for poetry to "be philosophical," a vital recognition is gained regarding the historical subordination of poetry to philosophy. Santayana considered his modern philosophic forebears and peers to be "like children playing blind-man's-buff; they are keenly excited at not knowing where they are."[44] They are "excited," one infers, because within the narrow parameters of their outlook the prospect of discovery seems to traditional Western philosophers endless. Reversing Socrates's challenge, a philosophy that could be proven to be "not only insightful, but beneficial" would surely be one that draws on the poet's power to *fling his soul upon the growing gloom*.

Notes

1. "There is an old quarrel between philosophy and poetry" (*Republic*, 607b5–6). All *Republic* citations C.D.C. Reeve translation (Hackett Publishing Company, 2004).

2. 607b.
3. 606d-5.
4. "[I]f Homer had really been able to educate people and make them better, if he'd known about these things and not merely about how to imitate them, wouldn't he have had many companions and been loved and honored by them? . . . do you suppose that, if Homer had been able to benefit people and make them more virtuous, his companions would have allowed either him or Hesiod to wander around as rhapsodes" (600c-d). These rhetorical questions of Socrates to Glaucon are meant to argue: Homer (and Hesiod) were obviously useless as educators, as seen in certain biographical facts, in the fact that they were allowed to wander around as "rhapsodes" and were not loved/sought after for private instruction, as for example Pythagoras (600b) was to develop a "way of life."
5. 602c.
6. For a stimulating analysis of this point see Glenn Most, "What Ancient Quarrel Between Philosophy and Poetry?" In the anthology *Plato and the Poets*. Brill Publishing, 2011. Edited by Pierre Destrée and Fritz-Gregor Herrmann: 1–20. Most argues that Plato likely invented this quarrel and that readers should interpret Socrates's pronouncement in terms other than historical.
7. Thomas Gould. *The Ancient Quarrel Between Poetry and Philosophy.* Princeton University Press, 1990.
8. Gould provides many provocative supplemental interpretations as to how the development of Christianity was "infected" with this Platonic influence.
9. For a perceptive criticism of Gould's thesis see the review by Stephen G. Salkever, Bryn Mawr College. *Bryn Mawr Classical Review*, 1991.03.12 (https:// bmcr.brynmawr.edu/1991/1991.03.12). Salkever sees Gould as engaging in a "grand reduction of complex and ambiguous philosophy to straightforward sectarian religious controversy." While I would agree that Gould's treatment amounts to *something* like this "reduction," given the depth of Gould's interpretive understanding there is more license in his reduction than Salkever acknowledges. As my invocation of Gould here illustrates, certain "reductive" critical enterprises provide provocations valuable enough on their own to make up for meantime interpretive distortions because they "edify" in exactly the sense expressed by Richard Rorty who argues that such interpretations maintain a conversation rather than purport to deliver objective truth. Gould's provocation ensures that the conversation over Plato's quarrel continues across centuries.
10. For example: Michel Foucault's view that Plato's views replaced a conception of truth "precious and desirable" in the age of Hesiod with what became in the Western tradition a preoccupation of truth "linked to the exercise of power" ("The Discourse on Language") has obvious parallels with Gould's view that knowledge of God became under the persuasion of Platonism beholden to human reason. And as I indicate in what follows, Gould's view of Plato's quarrel intersects with the critique of Stanley Rosen, itself overlapping with Nietzsche's view (which Jacques Lacan extended) that "Platonism . . . turned *against* nature, the body and its senses, and thus eventually against our capacities for a creative, flourishing life" (Tim Themi. *Lacan's Ethics and Nietzsche's Critique of Platonism.* SUNY Press, 2014: 7).
11. Gould, x.

12. "The moralism of the Greek philosophers from Plato downwards is pathologically conditioned," Friedrich Nietzsche. "The Problem of Socrates." In *Twilight of the Idols*, Penguin Classics, 1983. Translated by R.J. Hollingdale: 33.
13. Nietzsche, 33 (section 10). Echoing versions of this Nietzschean criticism can be found in the work of, among others, Max Horkheimer (1895–1973) and Michel Foucault (1926–1984)—their version of the critique centers on the notion of enlightenment rationality.
14. Thomas Hardy, winter poem "The Darkling Thrush."
15. Gould, xv.
16. Readers here should appreciate the important shift of consideration I am making from the epic style of poetry found in ancient times to this consideration of the lyric style that is that of the vernacular poetry in Dante's age.
17. Among other things, the piece effectively defends Dante's having written the "Divine Comedy" in Italian.
18. *De Vulgari Eloquentia* was written in Latin.
19. And indeed, the nature of Plato's banishment of poetry in his *Republic* should not be presumed to be understood, for example, as William Gahan observes in Chapter 5 of this book: "Sir Philip Sidney contends (1595) . . . that Plato's ousting of the poets in *The Republic* was misunderstood." (pg. 56).
20. Stanley Rosen. *The Quarrel Between Philosophy and Poetry*. Routledge, 1988: 109.
21. He contends that a woman's reproductive "prime" lasts for 20 years and a man's 30; a man's last chance to produce children is at age 55 when he reaches his "peak as a runner" (460e).
22. Rosen cross-connects an exchange between Glaucon and Socrates in the *Republic* at 458d5 with an exchange between Socrates and Agathon at *Symposium* 175e1.
23. Rosen, 116.
24. Rosen, 117.
25. Seth Benardete. *The Rhetoric of Morality and Philosophy*. University of Chicago Press, 2009: 142.
26. Silke-Maria Weineck. *The Abyss Above: Philosophy and Poetic Madness in Plato, Hölderlin, and Nietzsche*. SUNY Press, 2002: 34.
27. Ibid.
28. My subsequent chapter will discuss Heidegger's preoccupation with German Romantic poet Friedrich Hölderlin (1770–1843).
29. Variant of *poiétés,* from *poein, poiein* "to make."
30. Emphasis mine. George Santayana. *Interpretations of Poetry and Religion*. Critical Edition, co-edited by William G. Holzberger and Herman J. Saatkamp, Jr. The MIT Press, Cambridge, 1989: 171.
31. Spanish classical American philosopher George Santayana (1863–1952) was known for his philosophical system as equally as his career as a poet, novelist, and literary-poetic sensibility. He was also a first-rate cultural critic and prodigious interpreter of Christian history and religion (a late-career work titled *The Idea of Christ in the Gospels* displays Santayana's authoritative appreciation of biblical tradition and the cultural vitality of Christianity).
32. Griswold, Charles L., "Plato on Rhetoric and Poetry", The Stanford Encyclopedia of Philosophy (Spring 2020 Edition), Edward N. Zalta (ed.), URL = <https://plato.stanford.edu/archives/spr2020/entries/plato-rhetoric/>.
33. T.S. Eliot. *The Sacred Wood: Essays on Poetry and Criticism*. New York: Barnes & Noble Inc., 1959: 100.

34. Although the characterization is conventionally accepted, in the final chapter of this book I specify my opposition to the term "postmodern" in relation to Heidegger. I am similarly inclined against the characterization for Dewey and Wittgenstein.
35. Rorty termed them "edifiers."
36. "Truth as correspondence" is the idea that the truth of a statement is established by the accuracy with which it matches up with an objective external world/ reality. In *Philosophy and the Mirror of Nature*, Rorty's central argument is that philosophy needs to abandon the metaphor of mind as a medium of appearances that sorts them into categories of "mere"/false versus "reality"/truth-corresponding. The abandonment of truth-as-correspondence opens philosophy, in Rorty's view, to the opportunity to "re-describe" and engage in edifying conversations (as opposed to ceaseless argument).
37. In his "Apology" Socrates claims he saw through the poet's interpretive pretensions: "I saw that, because of their poetry, they thought themselves very wise men in other respects, which they were not" (22c). The "other respects" in which poets, according to Socrates, saw themselves wise was in their pretense to grasp higher truths.
38. Raymond Barfield. *The Ancient Quarrel between Philosophy and Poetry*. Cambridge University Press, 2011: 253.
39. Italics mine. William James. "Pluralism, Pragmatism, and Instrumental Truth." In *A Pluralistic Universe*: "nothing includes everything, or dominates over everything. The word 'and' trails along after every sentence. Something always escapes. 'Ever not quite' has to be said of the best attempts made anywhere in the universe at attaining all-inclusiveness" (Essays in *Radical Empiricism and Pluralistic Universe*, Longman's, Green and Co., 1943: 321).
40. Gould, xvi.
41. Bringing to mind the repeated line whose exact origin is (fittingly) unknown, that a poem is never finished but only abandoned.
42. William S. Allen. *Ellipsis Of Poetry and the Experience of Language After Heidegger, Holderlin, and Blanchot*. SUNY Press, 2008: 175.
43. Santayana, George. *Three Philosophical Poets Lucretius, Dante, and Goethe*, co-edited by Kellie Dawson and David E. Spiech. Introduction by James Seaton. Critical Edition, Volume VIII, *The Works of George Santayana*. The MIT Press, Cambridge, Massachusetts, and London, England, 2019: 7.
44. Santayana, George. *Soliloquies in England and Later Soliloquies*. Charles Scribner's Sons, 1922: 210.

References

Allen, William S. *Ellipsis: Of Poetry and the Experience of Language After Heidegger, Holderlin, and Blanchot*. SUNY Press, 2008.

Barfield, Raymond. *The Ancient Quarrel between Philosophy and Poetry*. Cambridge University Press, 2011.

Dante. *De Vulgari Eloquentia*. Edited and translated by Steven Botterill. Cambridge University Press, 1996.

Eliot, T.S. *The Sacred Wood: Essays on Poetry and Criticism*. Barnes & Noble Inc., 1959.

Gould, Thomas. *The Ancient Quarrel Between Poetry and Philosophy*. Princeton University Press, 1990.

Hardy, Thomas. *Selected Poems.* Edited and with an Introduction by Robert Mezey. Penguin Books, 1998.

James, William. *Essays in Radical Empiricism and A Pluralistic Universe*. Longman's, Green and Co., 1943.

Most, Glenn. "What Ancient Quarrel Between Philosophy and Poetry?" In *Plato and the Poets*. Editors Pierre Destrée and Fritz-Gregor Herrmann. Brill Publishing, 2011: 1–20.

Nietzsche, Friedrich. *Twilight of the Idols.* Translated by R.J. Hollingdale. Penguin Classics, 1983.

Plato. *Republic.* Translated from the New Standard Greek Text, with Introduction, by C.D.C Reeve. Hackett Publishing Company, 2004.

Rorty, Richard. *Philosophy and the Mirror of Nature*. Princeton University Press, 1979.

Rosen, Stanley. *The Quarrel Between Philosophy and Poetry*. Routledge, 1988.

Salkever, Stephen G. "Review of Gould, *The Ancient Quarrel Between Poetry and Philosophy.*" *Bryn Mawr Classical Review* (online): 1991.03.12 (https://bmcr.brynmawr.edu/1991/1991.03.12).

Santayana, George. *Interpretations of Poetry and Religion*. Critical Edition, co-edited by William G. Holzberger and Herman J. Saatkamp, Jr. The MIT Press, 1989—*Soliloquies in England and Later Soliloquies*. Charles Scribner's Sons, 1922.

Seth, Benardete. *The Rhetoric of Morality and Philosophy*. University of Chicago Press, 2009.

Themi, Tim. *Lacan's Ethics and Nietzsche's Critique of Platonism*. SUNY Press, 2014.

Weineck, Silke-Maria. *The Abyss Above: Philosophy and Poetic Madness in Plato, Hölderlin, and Nietzsche*. SUNY Press, 2002.

2 Vergil and Broch in Worlds Upside Down

Living the Quarrel Between Poetry and Philosophy

Stephanie Quinn

Does art speak the truth or tell lies, especially about history? Hermann Broch's[1] novel, *The Death of Virgil*, relies on an ancient biographical tradition regarding the Roman poet Vergil[2] (70–19 BCE). According to that tradition, Vergil's will instructed his executors to destroy his epic poem, the *Aeneid*, but the emperor Augustus intervened for its preservation (Otis 1964, 1). Vergil's doubts about his work became grist for Broch's (1886–1951 CE) reflection on the value of his art and of any art to tell the truth, especially in grave historical times. The problem confronted by these two artists was anticipated in Plato's *Republic* approximately 300 years before Vergil: the quarrel between poetry and philosophy, as explored in this volume.

Vergil's and Broch's explorations of this issue occur within two of the most significant periods in Western history—in Rome the transition from the Roman Republic to the Roman Empire in the late first century BCE, and, in Europe, the collapse of a world of empires, before, in, and between two world wars in the early twentieth century CE. In those two eras, the world stopped making sense to many people. Values and ideas that were assumed to be fixed and true seemed instead to be turned upside down. Questions about truth and reality were part of lived experience in both times.

The novel occupies about 500 pages of largely stream of consciousness narrative. The opening depicts a lovely scene in Brundisium (modern Brindisi, Italy), and the drama of the emperor Augustus's ship arriving in port. His ship carried Vergil "and death's signet was graved upon his brow."[3] The poet was suffering from seasickness and a "plaguing cough," as he lay with "ebbing consciousness" wondering:

> why then had he yielded to the importunity of Augustus? Why then had he forsaken Athens? Fled now the hope . . . for a life free alike of art and poetry, a life dedicated to meditation and study in the city of Plato . . . fled the hope for the *miracle of knowledge and the healing through knowledge.*
>
> (*DoV* 12, emphasis added)

Thus, according to Broch, does one of the greatest poets of the Western tradition, said by some to have defined that tradition,[4] refuse, or reveal his desire to have refused his art in favor of the city of Plato and the healing of knowledge. Why had he come to renounce poetry in favor of the world of philosophy?

> Nothing availed the poet, he could right no wrongs; he is heeded only if he extols the world, never if he portrays it as it is. . . . Oh yes, people would praise [the *Aeneid*], because only the agreeable things would be abstracted from it, and because there was neither danger nor hope that the exhortations would be heeded; ah, he was forbidden either to delude himself or to permit himself to be deluded.
>
> (*DoV* 15)

The problem of art's truth or its delusion, its use and misuse by others despite the poet's warnings, are attributed to Vergil from the outset and form the problem of Broch's novel, as they have formed the problem of Vergil scholarship for decades.

For Vergil, Broch, and here Broch's Vergil, the "quarrel" is part of lived experience.

> These were the masses for whom Caesar had lived, for which the empire had been established . . . these were the masses for whom the great peace of Augustus had been made.
>
> (*DoV* 22)

Broch's Vergil responds to the masses that greeted the emperor Augustus and tries to understand his response.

> but something new arose in him, something of which . . . he had never wanted to take cognizance . . . something that here in Brundisium had unexpectedly obtruded itself, namely the awareness of the people's profound capacity for evil.
>
> (*DoV* 23)

The novelist wrote some of this work while imprisoned for several months by the Nazis in Vienna during the Anschluss of March 1938, anticipating his own likely, imminent death.[5] Thereafter, Broch's late years were spent as a refugee in the United States. The ancient history referenced in the modern novel reflects decades of Roman blood shed by Romans in seemingly interminable fratricide in the first century BCE, not unlike Europe's half century of intra-European destruction. For most of his life, Vergil witnessed the disruptions that marked those Roman decades, although his poetic career was ultimately supported by a patron, Maecenas, one of Augustus's inner circle of advisers. Was Vergil then an Augustan propagandist, or was he a subtle but brave critic of the regime? Or both?[6] Both Vergil and Broch had lived virtually all their lives amidst evidence of human depravity, people's profound capacity for evil. Each anguished over his role as an artist in such a world.

In this chapter, I offer an overview of ancient Roman history at the fall of the Republic and beginning of the Empire plus some reports on conditions in twentieth-century Europe before and especially between the two world wars, of worlds upside down. With that background, I review contemporary reactions to those histories, the awareness of living in times of crisis, viewed even in their own times as historical turning points. The next section presents the uses that the modern period made of the ancient one across two millennia,[7] and in particular of Vergil himself; in other words, the context in which Broch came to know and choose Vergil's life and work as an effective platform.

Vergil and Broch explore and confront an ethical and philosophical question—the truth or falseness in history's use of art, how to say true things in real time, or, stated another way, the quarrel between poetry and philosophy. My second chapter in this volume explores Vergil's and Broch's responses to the quarrel.

Worlds Upside Down: Vergil's Rome and Broch's Europe

Both Vergil and Broch lived in times of historic crisis. For Vergil it was the fall of the 500-year-old Roman Republic (in the city then over 700 years old)[8] and with it the collapse of virtually all of the Republic's previously successful political and social institutions. This occurred through successive waves of civil conflict and outright civil war, Roman against Roman, severed heads of friends and family in the Forum (among them the orator Cicero's), state-authorized bloodshed within a small oligarchy in the streets of the city and abroad.[9] For Broch, it was the transition from the late nineteenth to early twentieth centuries, the Russian Revolution, the end of the Austro-Hungarian empire, the German loss of two wars in less than 30 years, the perceived failures of the Weimar democracy and culture and subsequent rise of extreme political parties on the right and left, the evidence of accelerating brutality and madness.[10] It was a time of pervasive stress, upheaval, confusion.

Many artists in these two eras were aware of the grand scale of their confusions. Johnson says of the *Aeneid*, "we are no longer sure what battles have been lost or what battles have been won" (1981, 55). In similar vein about the modern period, Schorske (1981, 116) quotes a novelist contemporary with Broch,

> People who were not born then, wrote Robert Musil of the Austrian *fin de siècle*, will find it difficult to believe, but . . . time was moving faster than a cavalry camel. . . . Nor . . . could anyone quite distinguish between what was . . . moving forward and what backward.

The similarities in tone among such commentators are striking.

The crisis at Rome called into question the values of republican life, especially for the ruling group, values of liberty, rational discourse, manly courage, trustworthiness to fellow citizens, the meaning of Rome itself. For Europeans, the coming turn of millennia called into question (and continues to do) the assumptions and values of the Enlightenment, of liberalism, reason, authority, questions, and perspectives expressed variously through the works of such figures as Picasso, Stravinsky, Diaghilev, Joyce, and the time- and energy-crushing science of Einstein.[11]

The resolution of Rome's crisis took about 100 years. It consisted of no less than the death of the Roman Republic and the birth of the system to support the Roman Empire, that is, a system for rule of the entire ancient Mediterranean world by a first leader, a *princeps*, a role that had early marks of and emerged into that of emperor. That transition was a revolution.[12] It consisted of fluid and dangerous allegiances among the ruling elites; the dominance of charismatic generals, with large followings of armed soldiers dependent on their leaders for their entire livelihood; skilled generals who feared no rules or conventions, however venerable their origins; and ultimately the virtual annihilation of the extended ruling families who had created the Republic and forged its success over centuries but who could not conceive its future. It was all confusion; it was a terrifying time.[13]

This period in Rome (first century BCE) has been characterized as "upside down," chaotic, contradictory: "Rome's traditions were denied . . . every aspect of Roman society was thrown into chaos."[14]

Not only society but the naming of reality itself apparently was contested.

> Wars dominated the era; victories were repeatedly gained—or claimed. That distinction is important. The humbling of external foes was a prime catchword of the regime. But the *difference between rhetoric and reality* is a central feature of the Augustan years, and of imperial policy. "[R]epresentation and reality often diverged."
>
> (Gruen 1990, 395, emphasis added)

Imagine the artist working in a time when the difference between rhetoric and reality was an everyday concern. What is an artist to do, what is art to be? Vergil and some contemporary Romans knew that they did not know:

> What sets/them apart from the previous generation of [Roman writers] is perhaps not a sense of foreboding that the inherited system could not maintain itself much longer, but a realization that some fundamental change was actually under way, the full import of which could not yet be predicted. This places the poets of the 30s and 20s BC in a truly liminal position.
>
> (Farrell and Nelis 2013, 4–5)

Just as these authors say that the Roman poets' "*consciousness* of this problem" (7, their emphasis) is the subject of their book, so is the mutual, intertextual if you wish,[15] consciousness of the problem shared by Vergil and Broch the subject of my essays here.

Vergil and Broch share a similar perception. Broch

> portrayed through his efforts over the next several years [after 1929] the causes for a general disintegration of value systems in the West and developed *Die Schlafwandler* [his novel *The Sleepwalkers*] into a massive work both looking back at the upheavals of two previous generations, and pointing ahead to an uncertain future.
>
> (Bernheim 1980, 59)

As Broch wrote (2002, 177), "In the nineteenth century, the dwindling of the old European system of beliefs had begun . . . [t]he universality of the governing ethical attitudes began to disintegrate." Broch "tolls out the old dead myths of culture; he rings in the new" (Lipking 1981, 134) including the myth of Vergil himself, as Vergil had done in reworking the Homeric models in ways both pellucidly recognizable and with revolutionary difference, towards an unknown but somehow palpably intuited future. Broch's doubts, voiced through his Vergil, and Vergil's doubts voiced by Broch are a rational response to irrationality. But where does that leave truth? Plato's quarrel between poetry and philosophy is not an abstraction for citizens, soldiers, and artists in such times.

Millennialism Across Millennia

To understand their eras, people sought the present in the past. Rome looked back to its mythic founding and even farther back to the already ancient tradition of a prior golden age. Parts of Europe, 2,000 years after Vergil, looked back to ancient Rome.

One resonance between *The Death of Virgil* and the *Aeneid* is the shared contemporary understandings of their own periods as enormously significant, from something known and largely horrible to something else, gleaned by some to be a good, by others not, but certainly on a world-historical scale, across great spans of time. Both eras took an almost mystical turn to the distant past to reinterpret and refound the present for the future. For both eras Vergil's works and especially the *Aeneid*, however interpreted— as glorification of empire or warning of its moral failure—were often a touchstone. Just as John Burns describes La Malincha in Chapter 4 here as a shifting mirror, so Vergil's works have reflected their readers' assumptions and needs across time.

For the Augustans themselves, several events signaled not just change but cyclical return with mystical meaning. Vergil's fourth *Eclogue* was largely responsible for his later reputation as foreseeing the coming of a religious savior. That poem describes the birth of a child and the consequent return to a previously extinct golden age.[16]

In the years before and after the 39–38 BCE publication of the *Eclogues*, politics at Rome continued in unsettled alliances. The culminating event came at the Battle of Actium in 31 BCE between Octavian (later named Augustus) and his allies versus Mark Antony and his, including Queen Cleopatra of Egypt. Interpretations of this battle vary, but there seems no doubt that it was decisive in eliminating any opposition to Octavian (Gurval 1995, 279). After 31, he ruled Rome.

Actium not only secured Octavian in power; the battle was interpreted, at the time or later, as the end of the century of civil warfare and, crucially, as the start of a new and better era, becoming the "foundation myth of the new order."[17] The paradoxical program of the new sole ruler, by the time of his death in 14 CE virtually an autocratic emperor, was to restore the republican polity of free citizens, to restore the republic, *restituere rem publicam* (Hardie 1993, 5).

In the tumult of Europe's war years 2,000 years later, Europeans, imbued in Roman history and literature, readily perceived analogies across the millennia. Theirs was a world in crisis, empires collapsing and institutions failing, multitudes dying in battle and of disease, rapid change in customs and mores, simultaneous worlds of opposite realities.

The quest in this period to make meaning reached back to Rome for models and sometimes for warning: "Ever since Spengler's *Der Untergang des Abendlandes* [*The Decline of the West*, in its familiar English title], analogies between the cultural and social crises of the early twentieth century and the Roman Empire have been popular" (Heizmann 2003, 188). Broch himself perceived "a parallel between his own century and the first century before Christ, both being epochs of radical change" (Heizmann 2003, 194). Lipking (1981, 131) cites Broch's statement on "the parallels between the first pre-Christian century and our own—civil war, dictatorship, and a dying away of the old religious forms."

For early twentieth-century Italians, relating to the city at the heart of that old empire, the connection between past and present must have been irresistible (although the nature of the analogy was a choice). Here is a statement by Mussolini published on April 21, 1922, April 21 being the traditional date for the founding of Rome in 753 BCE.

> Rome is our starting point and our point of reference; it is our symbol or, if you will, our myth. We dream of a Roman Italy: one/which is wise and strong, disciplined and imperial. Much of the immortal spirit of Rome is born again in fascism.
>
> (Kelly 2006, 122–123)[18]

Mussolini put on a great exhibition of Romanness to commemorate the 2,000th anniversary of the birth of Augustus, the *Mostra Augustea della Romanitá* (Augustan Exhibition of Romanness). The exhibition attracted a million visitors, among them Adolf Hitler, in May 1938. Hitler was inspired by Mussolini to advance his own efforts to rebuild Berlin, so that it should "be a city even more 'breathtaking' than Rome, 'our only rival in the world'" (Kelly 2006, 126).

The Roman connections sought and found in Germany were more than architectural. In Germany, the time between the two world wars was a period of "turmoil and insecurity, longing for fundamental change, longing for a *renovatio* [a renewing] to bring order and strength back to the political body" (Eiden 2006, 442). And in that time, there was apparently a "German fixation with Vergil. . . . Much of the interest focused on Augustus and the state" (Schmidt 2001, 150).

The millennial connections between Europe at the time and Augustan Rome were enhanced by and celebrated additionally through the commemorations of Vergil's birth, the bimillennium of which was marked in October 1930. Those connections were mixed regarding Vergil's meaning.

> In 1930 Europe celebrated the bimillennium of Virgil's birth. The celebrations fell in the middle of Mussolini's dictatorship (1922–43), strengthening the links that Mussolini sought to establish between his Italian regime and ancient Rome. The *Aeneid*, singing of the birth of a new city and a new empire, helped to validate Mussolini's imperialist policies, and in 1936 a new Italian empire was born. In the same year, the Austrian writer Hermann Broch began to meditate upon Virgil's position in the modern world and by 1937 he had conceived his novel *The Death of Virgil*.

The opposed political approaches to Virgil offered by Mussolini and the anti-Fascist Broch typify the variety of Virgilian studies proliferating at this time. A renaissance of interest in Virgil was due not solely to the bimillennium, but more suggestively to the sense of crisis pervading Europe in the *entre-deux-guerres* [between two wars] period.

(Cox 1997, 327)

Vergil was the location for celebrating the bimillennium of empire, of Christianity, and also of crisis. The appropriation of Vergil to celebrate one political outlook over another was an interpretative choice, then and now.

The uses of the *Aeneid* resulted from more than school days familiarity. The frequent modern European uses of the poem speak to essential aspects of the *Aeneid*, as a poem not only of empire achieved but also of exile, loss, the upside-down-ness of thwarted goals and perverted mission, in the name of founding empire. The poem speaks of:

mobility and communication across time and space. . . . At the level of the primary plot the poem is about a hero in transition between one home now lost, and another, whose fullest realization lies far beyond his own lifetime. The legendary passage between two worlds reflects the transition that Rome was undergoing in Virgil's own day between one political order and another.

(Hardie 2014, 145)

Centuries before Vergil, Aeneas, the *Aeneid*'s hero, and his fellow refugee Trojans of Homeric tradition battled the native Italians with whom they would centuries later share descendants and imperial glory. The *Aeneid* thus placed its contemporary readers in the position of looking back at their own founders in folly, confusion and ignorance, conditions they themselves were experiencing in their own founding of a world unknowable to them:

Vergil is also the European poet in whom, for the first time, we discover a new and epoch-making sense of historical time. Vergil is fascinated by people who feel lost in history, who are being propelled by forces they cannot understand toward a future from which they cannot escape.

(Most 2001, 189)

As I demonstrate in my second chapter in this volume, to read the *Aeneid* across millennia is to read it correctly.

Vergil and Broch knew what they could not fully know; for each, a whole world was coming to an end. This left each of them with only a limited way to say true things about himself and his life's work. The truest thing Vergil could do, that later Broch could do, was question the truth of what they were doing.[19] As history was marching on a grand scale, so was this questioning: "And if we do not have the courage to prove ourselves false, how shall we succeed in being honest."[20] If poetry fails, the questioning of it merges into the philosophical question, named since Plato, of the nature and possibility of truth itself, framed as a quarrel between poetry and philosophy.

Vergil's core question was not whether he was a proponent of Augustus or not, a good republican, or a blissful fan of the new order. The question was how to do his job, whether his job was ethically possible, and whether he should do it at all. These are also the issues for Broch's time, which he puts into his Vergil's mind in *The Death of Virgil*.

My subsequent chapter in this volume explores how the two authors respond to these problems and in so doing answer the quarrel. The Holocaust historian Saul Friedländer recommends a way to tell the truth of the Shoah: "The commentary should disrupt the facile linear progression of the narrative, introduce alternative interpretations, question the partial conclusion, withstand the need for closure" (Goldberg 2009, 228). Vergil and Broch already knew that. Friedländer urges historians to depict history in a way that seems more poetic than scientific. The experience of the Nazi regime was for many so extreme that its truth seemed inexpressible. What Friedländer recommends for history writing may or may not be possible for that profession. As we will see in my subsequent chapter, Vergil and Broch, I believe, found a way to do it in poetry.

Notes

1. For essays in English on Broch and his work, see Bartram *et al.* (2019).
2. The Latin name of the *Aeneid*'s poet is Publius Vergilius Maro. The history of the spellings of Vergil and Virgil relates to the Christianizing of Vergil's legacy, in which Vergil was seen as a prophet of a new figure and new age, a kind of magician. In Latin, the word for a magic stick or wand is *virga*, and it may be that the V-i-rgil spelling arose from that source. See Wilson-Okamura (2010).
3. *Death of Virgil* 3, hereafter *DoV*.
4. Eliot called the *Aeneid* "the classic of all Europe" (1957, 73).
5. See William Gahan's reference to the life-threatening situation of Boethius in Chapter 3.
6. See Johnson (1976, 15–16); Hardie (1993, 2); and also Schmidt (2001, 171): "Thus the *Aeneid* is at the same time both the deepest and most sublime representation of Rome as an idea and its most serious problematization."
7. For a range of essays on this topic, see Roche and Demetriou (2018).
8. Historical reminders: the traditional date for the founding of Rome is 753 BCE; for the founding of the Roman Republic, 509 BCE; Julius Caesar was

assassinated by several senators in 44 BCE (the Ides of March); Octavian, who had been adopted by Julius Caesar, defeated Antony and Cleopatra at the Battle of Actium in 31 BCE. Octavian received the title of "Augustus" in 27 BCE. That date is typically used as the start of the Roman Empire.

9. See notably Alston (2015, 142) on the proscriptions, that is, the lists of Romans to be killed, published by the triumvirate of Octavian (later Augustus), Mark Antony, and Lepidus.

10. "The Weimar period itself has been characterized by a host of traumata: the lost war, experienced as the humiliation of defeat; the Treaty of Versailles, imposed by the victors, often called in Germany 'the dictate of Versailles'; . . . All these wounds led many German intellectuals and patriots to crave an effective government, a powerful state, and the charismatic personality of a politician with vision and leadership qualities" (Schmidt 2001, 152). See generally Bergen (2016). I am grateful to my Rockford University colleague Dr. Edward Mathieu for this and other references.

11. Thank you to our colleague Dr. Deepshikha Shukla for help with this phrase.

12. For example, Syme (1939), *The Roman Revolution* and Alston (2015), *Rome's Revolution.*

13. For example, Julius Caesar, about the war between him and Pompey ending in Caesar's victory at the Battle of Pharsalus in 48 BCE: "The consuls left Rome without taking the auspices, another thing that never happened before that occasion, and used lictors in Rome in a private capacity, contrary to every precedent. . . . All rights, divine and human, were thrown into confusion" (*omnia divina humanaque iura permiscentur*) *Bellum Civile* 1.6, Damon (2016). Vergil was about 20 years old at the time. A student in my ancient Roman history course spontaneously said of this period, "This is terrifying." See also Johnson (1976, 15), the *Aeneid* "is a terrifying poem."

14. Alston (2015, 8) and Crawford (1993, Chapter XIII). See also Zanker's chapter (1990), "Conflict and Contradiction in the Imagery of the Dying Republic."

15. Please refer to note 8 in my subsequent chapter of this volume for references on theoretical issues in classical studies relevant to this project.

16. Along with nationalistic and fascistic readings of Vergil's works was a modern Christianizing reading, notably by Theodor Haecker, who found in Vergil's work a sensibility that he called an *anima naturaliter christiana*, "a spirit naturally Christian" (1934, 109). Cox (1997, 328) claims that "Haecker exerted an enormous influence upon Broch." The idea of Vergil presaging Christianity was not new of course; witness Dante. See also Eliot's "Vergil and the Christian World," 1953, which cites Haecker; also Lipking (1981, 222, n. 132).

17. Gurval (1995, 3 and 289), quoting Syme. See also Eck (2003, 40), "What everyone shared was a desire for peace, and many were prepared to pay a high price for it. When Octavian ordered the Temple of Janus Quirinus in Rome closed in 29 BC, to mark the return of peace to the entire Roman state, he intended it to symbolize the start of a new era."

18. See also for example Kallis (2011) and Ceci (2017).

19. I am reminded of Matthew Caleb Flamm's discussion of the *Phaedrus*, quoting Weineck: " poets who can critique their own work might be philosophers."

20. I am indebted to my friend and colleague Dr. Donald E. Martin for his translation of the novel *Leonis* by George Theotokas, where the lead character ends the novel, set just before World War I, with those words (1985, 145).

References

Alston, Richard. 2015. *Rome's Revolution: Death of the Republic and Birth of the Empire.* Oxford University Press.

Bartram, Graham, Sarah McGaughey, and Galin Tihanov, eds. 2019. *A Companion to the Works of Hermann Broch.* Camden House.

Bergen, Doris L. 2016. *War & Genocide: A Concise History of the Holocaust.* Rowman and Littlefield.

Bernheim, Mark. 1980. "Style: Abstraction and Empathy in Hermann Broch's *Die Schlafwandler* [*The Sleepwalkers*]." *Modern Austrian Literature*, 13.4, 59–76.

Broch, Hermann. 1995. *The Death of Virgil.* Translated by Jean Starr Untermeyer. Random House.

Broch, Hermann. 1996. *The Sleepwalkers.* Translated by Willa and Edwin Muir. Random House.

Broch, Hermann. 2002. "Hugo von Hofmannsthal and His Time: Art and Its Nonstyle at the End of the Nineteenth Century." In *Geist and Zeitgeist: The Spirit of an Unspiritual Age*, edited by John Hargraves. Counterpoint, 141–210.

Ceci, Lucia. 2017. *The Vatican and Mussolini's Italy.* Brill.

Cox, Fiona. 1997. "Envoi: The Death of Virgil." In *The Cambridge Companion to Virgil*, edited by Charles Martindale. Cambridge, 327–336.

Crawford, Michael. 1993. *The Roman Republic*, second edition. Harvard University Press.

Damon, Cynthia. 2016. *Julius Caesar, Civil War.* Harvard University Press.

Eck, Werner. 2003. *The Age of Augustus.* Translated by Deborah Lucas Schneider. Blackwell.

Eiden, Patrick. 2006. "*Translatio imperii ad Americam.* Working Through the Poetics of Empire in Hermann Broch's *The Death of Virgil*." *Literary Imagination*, 8.3, 441–66.

Eliot, T.S. 1953. "Vergil and the Christian World." *The Sewanee Review*, 61.1 (Winter), 1–14.

Eliot, T.S. 1957. "What is a Classic?" In *On Poetry and Poets.* Farrar, Straus and Cudahy.

Faircough, Rushton H. 1994 and 1996. *Vergil I* and *Vergil II. Harvard.*

Goldberg, Amos. 2009. "The Victim's Voice and Melodramatic Aesthetics in History." *History and Theory*, 48.3 (October 2009), 220–237. Review of Saul Friedländer's 1997 *Nazi Germany and the Jews: The Years of Extermination.*

Gruen, Erich S. 1990. "The Imperial Policy of Augustus." In *Between Republic and Empire. Interpretations of Augustus and His Principate*, edited by Kurt Raaflaub and Mark Toher. California University Press, 395–416.

Gurval, Robert. 1995. *Actium and Augustus. The Politics and Emotions of Civil War.* Michigan University Press.

Haecker, Theodor. 1934. *Virgil: Father of the West.* Tranlsated by A.W. Wheen. Sheed & Ward.

Hardie, Philip. 1993. *The Epic Successors of Virgil: A Study of the Dynamics of a Tradition.* Cambridge University Press.

Hardie, Philip. 2014. *The Last Trojan Hero. A Cultural History of Virgil's Aeneid.* I.B. Tauris.

Heizmann, Jürgen. 2003. "A Farewell to Art: Poetic Reflection in Broch's Der Tod des Vergil." In *Hermann Broch, Visionary in Exile. The 2001 Yale Symposium,* edited by Paul Michael Lützeler. Camden House, 187–200.

Johnson, W. Ralph. 1976. *Darkness Visible. A Study of Vergil's* Aeneid. California University Press.

Johnson, W. Ralph. 1981. "The Broken World. Virgil and His Augustus." *Arethusa* 141, 49–56.

Kallis, Aristotle. "'Framing' *Romanitá*: The Celebrations for the *Bimillenario Augusteo* and the *Augusteo—Ara Pacis* Project." *JCH,* 46.4 (2011), 809–831.

Kelly, Christopher. 2006. *The Roman Empire: A Very Short Introduction.* Oxford University Press.

Lipking, Lawrence. 1981. *The Life of the Poet: Beginning and Ending of Poetic Careers.* Chicago University Press.

Most, Glenn. 2001. "Lacrimae Rerum: The influence of Vergil Virtual roundtable, with participation by Karl Kirchwey, J. D. McClatchy, Kenneth Haynes, Paul Alpers, Paul A. Cantor, Glenn Most, Margaret Anne Doody." In *Poets and Critics Read Vergil,* edited by Sarah Spence. Yale University Press, 189–91.

Otis, Brooks. 1964. *Virgil: A Study in Civilized Poetry.* Oxford University Press.

Roche, Helen and Kyriakos Demetriou, eds. 2018. *Brill's Companion to the Classics, Fascist Italy and Nazi Germany.* Brill.

Schmidt, Ernst. 2001. "The Meaning of Vergil's *Aeneid*: American and German Approaches." *CW,* 94.2, 145–171.

Schorske, Carl E. 1981. *Fin-de-Siècle Vienna. Politics and Culture.* Vintage Books, Random House.

Syme, Ronald. 1939. *The Roman Revolution.* Oxford University Press.

Theotokas, George. 1985. *Leonis: A Novel.* Translated by Donald E. Martin. A Nostos Book.

Wilson-Okamura, David Scott. 2010. *Virgil in the Renaissance.* Cambridge University Press.

Zanker, Paul. 1990. *The Power of Images in the Age of Augustus.* Translated by Alan Shapiro. Michigan University Press.

3   Lessons, Lies, and Legacies

The Place of Poetry in Thomas More's *Utopia* and Philip Sidney's *Defense of Poesy*

William Gahan

Poetry (widely defined as imaginative works) was variously approached as an important element of society and the formation of early modern identity. In this chapter, I discuss the perceived place of poetry in relation to philosophy in famous medieval and early modern texts that grapple with Plato's pronouncement. Namely, Boethius's *Consolation of Philosophy*, a sixth-century Roman text translated by "King Alfred," Chaucer, and Queen Elizabeth I;[1] Thomas More's *Utopia* (1516); and Sir Philip Sidney's *Defense of Poesy* (1579, published in 1595). These last two evince a keen consciousness of the ways power dynamics, biases, and the indeterminacy of language affect attitudes regarding imaginative thinking.

If Plato's distrust of poetry was not shared by many early modern writers, his desire to build a state based on virtuous character was. For Plato, kicking out the poets abetted his plan in the *Republic*. Many early modern thinkers saw poetry as necessary for nurturing and cultivating virtue and proper rule. Italian humanist and poet Petrarch (1304–1374) strove to achieve spiritual and psychological transcendence through poetry in the fourteenth century. Not only this. As James Hankins shows in *Virtue Politics*, Petrarch's literary endeavors were part of a project to save Italy and even all of Christendom. Humanism was still seen as an antidote to greed and immoral expediency in sixteenth-century Europe: Baldassare Castiglione's Italian *Courtier* (1529) set forth instructions for counseling a monarch through the artful conveyance of ideals, and it was quickly translated into several languages; Sir Hoby's English translation was published in 1561.[2]

As will be discussed here, Thomas More's *Utopia* (1516) uses poetry and creative idealism in its presentation of the unreal but idealized land of Utopia as well as the character who describes it, Raphael Hythloday ("peddler of nonsense" in Greek). Thomas More (1478–1535), at least early in the text, insists (through a character with his own name) that this spokesman serve monarchs by counseling good behavior and moral leadership in a world of Machiavellian statecraft.

It is characteristic of More to suggest this. *Utopia* explores the value of compromise and the need for "poetic" idealism in a dangerously cutthroat world. It is relevant at any time, but it is not difficult to see how More's historical circumstances fit his interests. More was a leading humanist of his day and Chancellor to Henry VIII. Famously, More defended Catholicism against reformers until he had to choose between King and God. In 1535, he was executed for refusing to take the Oath of Supremacy acknowledging Henry as head of the English church.

Like More, Sir Philip Sidney (1554–1586) was a strong-willed believer (though on the Protestant side). He famously fought against Catholics and died in battle. Both men wielded imaginative writing as well as action to explore their ideals and defend them in a volatile world. If More's *Utopia* suggests that ennobling counsel and examples are necessary in court, Sidney's *Defense of Poesy* (published 1595), argues that poetry offers virtuous examples for emulation. How do these early modern writers diverge from Plato's attitude about poetry as seen in the *Republic*? In the following pages, I attempt to shed some light on this question.

If art and poetry are involved in "making" while philosophy is engaged in "discovery," then each of the previous texts can be read to show how both "making" and "discovering" are separate aspects of the same endeavor, both in ruminations regarding public policy and in the fashioning of identity.[3] Why was this distinction between imaginative creation and philosophical discovery seen as so important by Plato in the *Republic*? For Plato's *Republic*, the imaginative arts moved the passions and suggested immoral ideas and behaviors contrary to those the guardians of the state were entrusted to uphold. Through Socratic playfulness and perhaps irony, Socrates and Glaucon "discover" a republic built upon an originary lie whose consequences were intended to promote particular virtues.[4] Poetry and philosophy differ in their approach towards truth. For example, did Homer really believe a Cyclops existed as a flesh and blood monster? Or are his depictions poetic ways to convey minatory influences with which humans all grapple? As Philip Sidney famously notes in his *Defense*, poetry does not lie because it "nothing affirms."

To use Griswold's language, the assumption behind "discovering" is that there exists an essential and stable truth. But stable truths are elusive at best in the realm of human emotions, the mysteries of life, and the indeterminacy of language. Plato's penchant for mathematical concepts attests to his distrust of language: how could something so slippery as language lead one to a clear apprehension of his *ideas*? In the *Republic* at least, poetry should not be used to abet their discovery because (for Plato) it occludes a vision of the perfect forms. But Plato's *ideas* themselves are poetic creations. Socrates and Glaucon creatively "discover" a state that upholds certain ideas of virtue by way of guardians, raised on targeted lies about their literally autochtho-nous birth. This concocted Earthly origin, which Plato admits to be a salu-tary "lie," suggests an ironic awareness that the expressed original source is posited poetically.[5]

As we shall see, Thomas More mischievously pretends Utopia is a real place, and the winking is quite elaborate—even on the scale of a playful conspiracy among his friends. Sir Philip Sidney begins his essay ironically with suggestions that personal bias colors the truth and ends with a mock curse that belies awareness in the untrustworthiness of language. These early modern texts are more up-front about the poetic nature of "discover-ing" than the Plato of the *Republic* was.

Another reason Plato barred poets is that their "making" may run counter to his already-"discovered" program for a model state in the *Republic*; poets may disrupt further discovery of knowledge and the pursuit of goodness sanctioned by the guardians. Plato's ideal republic privileges "poetic" think-ing only from philosopher-kings.[6] Another distinction between sanctioned and illegitimate poetic activity is found in Medieval Christian philosophical texts that praise poetry stemming from Biblical sources. The Stoic Lady Philosophy in Boethius's *The Consolation of Philosophy* sings in verse that is legitimized only insofar as it serves to reconcile emotions to a Christian Stoic vision of the cosmos. And early modern NeoPlatonists praise poetry from churchmen and aristocratically-minded courtiers and scholars. Even iconoclastic seventeenth-century Puritans privilege poetic expressions from their versions of the Hebrew Scriptures and books of the New Testament. (Puritans of this period believed the Church of England was too "Catholic," and they rejected any symbols, icons, poetry, plays, behaviors, or rituals that they saw as contrary to the Ten Commandments.)[7]

Boethius's sixth-century *The Consolation of Philosophy*, written while facing execution, was prized across the middle ages for over 400 years. Boethius was a Roman senator who claims he was falsely accused of trea-son and sorcery, for which he was imprisoned and then executed in 524 or 525.[8] I include it here because it was immensely popular in early modern England (Queen Elizabeth composed her own translation). Its approach to questions of good and evil, fortune, predestination, and free will—as well as its concomitant stoic remedies for suffering—were popular for both medi-eval thinkers and early modern readers. In line with the antipoetic prej-udice introduced by Plato, *The Consolation* marshals forth a personified Philosophy to banish the Muse of Poetry. But what is actually banished is Boethius's emotional, poetic outpouring of lament and suffering. Poetry that furthers the delivery of philosophical endurance is used throughout. And as Victor Watts points out regarding the "philosophical basis" of the *Consola-tion*: "The scheme is undoubtedly Platonic."[9]

Further, personifying Philosophy is already an obvious poetic device. The trajectory to enlightenment follows a series of prose dialogues hewn together by poetic interludes. Lady Philosophy herself provides these poetic hymns for various purposes, some to help bridge an emotional and intellectual gap between Boethius's feelings of betrayal by his political adversaries and his desire to find solace in the justice of providence. Songs and poetry fashion a balm that helps Boethius reconcile his feelings about being unjustly condemned with what Lady Philosophy tries to teach: she wants Boethius to (re)discover that his sufferings are due to a forgetfulness and misunderstanding regarding the just workings of God. Here, imaginative writing, far from detracting its object from truth, serves a healing purpose by bringing its listener closer to it.[10] This truth is in line with the prevailing Christian Stoicism (which rejected slavery to passion and taught adherence to God), both at the time of its writing and in medieval and early modern England.

More and Sidney, centuries after Plato and Boethius, differ from them by consciously treating poetry only as a tool used in all forms of persuasion and expression. And they go further: poetic devices and imaginative thinking abet the apprehension of virtue and justice through the positing of salutary examples.

Sir Thomas More's *Utopia* is replete with irony and playfulness, while ostensibly couching its persuasion in classical rhetorical form. He writes a fictional piece about the limitations of human endeavors to govern ideally. *Utopia* suggests that storytelling and imagination are salutary. They provide a fulcrum from which to evaluate present circumstances and effectuate change. In addition to pondering the place of intellectual endeavors in government, Thomas More's writings explore the uneasy relationship between "fictional" writing and "truthful" reporting in statecraft.

Surrounding the work are several letters and poems that further the playful dalliance between imaginative creation and philosophical inquiry. The author and his friends carry on a correspondence pretending that Utopia is an actual place, winking at each other as they dupe the more gullible readers. The work begins with a rhyme that says, "No-Place" (Utopia) can now "outdo" Plato's republic because *Utopia* is "drawn out" and "made live anew" whereas Plato "only drew" his in "empty words." He then adds that Utopia will be called "the Good Place."[11]

The rhyme calls to mind the punning of the name as both "no place" (*ou*-topia) and "good place" (*eu*-topia), and explicitly purports to surpass the *Republic* because it brings the place to life, while Plato could only talk about it. Upholding "showing" over "telling," More performs a playful defense of poetry.

While we smile with More at this, Dominic Baker-Smith may be right that "the *Republic* is not proffered as the blueprint for a realizable project but as a stimulus to private reflection and individual action." In turn, despite More's irony, "Utopia may offer a working model of a true commonwealth far more vivid in its realization than Plato's abstract proposals, but it still only exists in words."[12]

Both the *Republic* and *Utopia* are imaginative hypotheticals, but More's seems less uneasy about how the faculties of poetry and the discoveries of philosophy are necessarily entwined. The text critiques any exclusive reliance on only one or the other, in part by playfully mixing them on purpose. The biographical Thomas More is a cryptic persona written into the "novel," and this character writes to his friend Peter Giles, who is also a historical friend of the author, to discuss what the idealistic thinker Hythloday ("peddler of nonsense") had said to them about Utopia ("no place"). By the end of the second book, Hythloday is taken "by the hand" into court, as if he were a child ushered into an important adult's chamber of business.[13] More makes a fuss about the particulars of this made-up place as if they were factual and then admits he forgot to find out where it is. His closing letter to Peter Giles yet again playfully defends the factual "truth" of the report about Utopia in the face of one critic's need to know whether it is a true or false place.[14] All of this is part of the salutary mischief of a writer who knows that "discovering" always partakes of "making."

A central concern in *Utopia* is whether a contemplative and idealistic counselor like Raphael Hytholday should serve a king. Although "Hythloday" means "peddler of nonsense," "Raphael" represents a healer and a savior, recalling the archangel.[15] The first part of the text involves a discussion about how justice is inefficiently and unethically meted in England, and Hythloday keenly and trenchantly points them out, suggesting remedies; the second includes Hythloday's untrustworthy description of the marvels to be found in Utopia, including a society that purports to have stamped out greed and who uses gold for chamber pots and regular metal for more noble use.[16]

More is aware of the artistic flexibility, creativity, and acumen needed to navigate amid different biases, temperaments, and personalities in politics. As mentioned previously, he was beheaded in 1535 for not agreeing that Henry was the head of the English church; a man for all seasons, it is extraordinary that he lasted as long as he did in such a volatile court.[17] *Utopia* illustrates bias often: before hearing the narrative about Utopia, a skeptical friend of More's, Peter Giles, supposes it will be far-fetched, and declares that "people in that new land" are not "better governed than in the world we know. . . . Long experience has helped us develop many conveniences of life, and by good luck we have discovered many other things which human ingenuity could never have hit upon."[18] Time and again, the text highlights ways in which flawed individuals have difficulty seeing outside their own purview; distrusting the story he will hear about a new world somewhere in America, Giles privileges knowledge gleaned from familiar experience, which can potentially blind him to other ideas. Hythloday, in turn, is so enamored with his utopian society that he misses its inherent injustices and inconsistencies; his blindness regarding Utopia is inversely commensurate with his keen vision regarding the problems of early modern London described earlier.

In a worldly setting of varying biases and power imbalances, the character More argues against Hythloday's cynicism about the viability of a counselor such as himself improving policy in England. More also keeps Hythloday's idealism in check about the utopian outcomes of abolishing private property. For More, living by upright principles does not preclude flexibility in acting within an understanding of the many motivations of others. In other words, he is aware of contingent issues and of actors on the political stage. He knows that art is political, and politics partakes of artistic maneuvers towards more salutary ends: one must take an approach that "adapts itself to the drama in hand, and acts its part neatly and appropriately." The character More continues, "You must strive to influence policy indirectly, handle the situation tactfully, and thus what you cannot turn to good, you may at least make as little bad as possible." Regarding the responsibility to ennoble others, he adds, "It is impossible to make everything good unless you make all men good, and that I don't expect to see for a long time to come."[19]

Sir Philip Sidney's 1579 *Defense of Poesy*, which defines poetry as any imaginative creation, makes explicit what More performs: poetry can be a vehicle towards virtuous action.[20] In addition to others, he argues that Plato himself, Boethius, Vergil, and More all strive to achieve this high purpose. They embody the Horatian dictum to instruct while delighting, "which Plato and Boethius well knew, and therefore made Mistress Philosophy very often borrow the masking raiment of Poesy."[21] More importantly, they instruct by providing ideal examples of behavior for imitation: he asks who can teach virtue better than Vergil's Aeneas? Or "what philosopher's counsel can so readily direct a prince, as the feigned Cyrus in Xenophon?"[22] Sidney borrows from Aristotle in discussing the representational nature of poetry. It is also superior to history and philosophy precisely because it is free to imagine better ideals for emulation than can actual, particular examples to which history is tied.[23] Poetry has all of the advantages of the precepts of philosophy but also the ability to show them forth. For Sidney, the way Thomas More fashioned *Utopia* can potentially make readers visualize ideals and emulate them more successfully than can philosophical conjectures. This is because it is fully figured forth poetically, thence moving the will to reproduce the ideals and take action.[24] The good artist does not merely copy a copy, as Plato surmises in the *Republic*. Rather, the artist perceives the pure idea and manifests it in art. This activity creates a "new nature" by means of a speaking picture (*ut pictura poesis*) which serves to instruct and delight.[25] Is this not precisely what Plato was doing himself in the *Republic*?

Aware of the concern that if the arts, like all rhetoric, can lead the passions towards the emulation of the good, then they can also lead astray, as Plato feared. But Sidney argues that this is not the fault of art or poetry. Rather, it is the practitioner of the art whose intentions and abilities may not hit the mark.[26] More on this idea in the conclusion to the current chapter.

Long before modern linguistic theories and deconstruction, both More and Sidney belied an awareness of the differences between signifier and signified, of the slipperiness of language, and the need to be adaptable when applying ideals in the real world. As Risa Bear points out in her introduction to the *Defence of Poesie*, thinkers like Petrus Ramus, a French humanist of the sixteenth century, claimed that no givens can be found upon which to build syllogisms: instead, even the "original" ones are but posited. If, as Bear notes, Plato

> sought an immaterial reality, [and] Aristotle [sought] a material one, Sidney suspects that neither can be found by us, but at best a model of a posited model, or copy of a posited copy (Plato's nightmare) can be fashioned and tested.[27]

Plato's "posited reality" of the ideal state is built upon what he terms a salutary lie: the guardians are taught to believe they were born of the earth. For the *Republic* to succeed, the guardians and the people must all work together according to the enlightened program fostered by the philosopher kings. In this sense, Plato places a lot of stock on "nurturing" in order to create an ideal "nature," all through what can be seen as a poetic conjuration.

Like More, Sidney was aware of political motives and personal biases that influence arguments. His defense answers anyone who would denounce the imaginative arts.[28] To suggest the humorous ways that personal circumstances and predispositions influence points of view, he narrates how Jon Pietro Pugliano, Emperor Maximilian II's esquire, praises horsemanship above politics and all else because horsemanship is his favorite thing. Much as Sidney does for poetry more earnestly, here he nevertheless notes that every man lives according to his humor and that rhetoric can cast powerful spells: "if I had not been a piece of a Logician before I came to him, I think he would have persuaded me to have wished myself a horse." With the sophisticated nonchalance of an aristocrat raised to see poetic writing as a mere pastime, he says he "slipped into the title" of a poet, suggesting a horse slipping into a bridle, as if his "unelected vocation" dictated the form and content of his arguments.[29]

Sidney would not categorize as poetry any productions that do not aim to ennoble. And for art that doesn't succeed in doing this, Sidney cites the failings of individuals, not art itself: it is "the fault of the man, and not of the poet."[30] But, as was Thomas More, Sidney was also aware of the danger inherent in any powerful imaginative thinking. After all, art is a tool, and it can be used for good or ill. Surely with an oblique allusion to the Platonic (and Puritan) charge that poets cast spells, Sidney ends his argument with a tongue-in-cheek curse on all who do not believe him, mockingly lending credence to Puritan attacks on the evil and magical nature of poetic conjurations. At the same time, he forcefully points out that legacies are created through poetic, myth-making energies.[31]

The previous medieval and early modern texts, touchstones in the development of English identity through this phase of its history wherein vernacular literature adapted and adopted classical texts and ideas in its own ways, suggest the cognitive inseparability between imaginative thinking and other modes of intellectual inquiry. Plato's injunction in the *Republic* against imaginative thinking was somewhat less fraught in other traditions: In addition to the aforementioned humanist program of learning in early modern Europe, the Spaniards also saw poetry as essential for politics and nation-building. In a famous 1492 letter from the Spanish Antonio de Nebrija to the Queen of Spain, the writer affirms that poetry and language are the real tools of power in establishing any empire.[32]

More than 300 years later, the English Romantics saw poetry as a political and personal remedy against the errors of the Enlightenment: Percy Bysshe Shelley famously affirmed that poets are "the unacknowledged legislators of the world,"[33] and Charles and Mary Lamb saw the works of Shakespeare as exceedingly ennobling for all.[34] Twentieth-century Walter Benjamin, describing art's uses for capitalism after what he saw as the failure of the Enlightenment, pointed out that art has become ephemeral and ubiquitous, having lost its *aura*, now deracinated from tradition and ritual; eviscerated from its original meaning, but set free for culture to use for its own ends.[35] He and some of his Frankfurt School contemporaries like Theodor Adorno saw a sameness in the diversity of "pop art," which is, as Nato Thompson calls it, the "weapon" of modern day culture.[36]

The question of whether art "ennobles" is no longer popular in a postmodern world. Fifty years ago, Anthony Burgess's *A Clockwork Orange* proposed various ways even the most sublime music can inspire hateful actions. Today, in terms of power, what was once "high art" versus "low art" is turned upside down: Ballet, artistic fiction, and classical music are still seen as refined and maybe edifying, but popular music and media hold nearly all the cultural sway. On the other side of this dichotomy, the utilitarian push for STEM and business specializations downplay all art as useless.

In the United States, kindergarten teachers call children "creative," but the "serious" affairs of industry, statecraft, and politics are generally understood as separate from imaginative endeavors. If poetry and the humanities are derided as "untrue" and business and political considerations are upheld as closer to "reality," then what does it mean for a populist politician—who invents facts on the spot—to be seen by supporters as one who "tells it like it is"? Plato derided the power of poets but actually used poetic devices to advance his cause. In today's culture, the humanities are under siege while media and talking images reign supreme over distracted hearts and minds.

Of course, politicians and advertisers are not usually trying to ennoble—they use rhetoric and the arts as tools towards their own ends—whether the manipulation is good or bad depends on the skill and intention of the practitioners and the alertness of its consumers. If there is an antidote to negative manipulation, it may be, as ever, exposure and knowledge about how philosophy and art can inform our prevailing culture and politics.

As discussed in Chapter 5 on Shakespeare's sonnets, concerns about the place of art in our lived experiences, in our desires and our emotions, live on. Plato feared the indeterminacy of language to show forth his ideas faithfully, and he does not trust poets to convey them because he sees poetic invention as too far removed from their original. There will always be a need to tolerate ambiguity when the signifier can never absolutely equal the signified. As Stephanie Quinn points out with her discussion of the *chôra*, a place suggestive of the "*ou*-topia," or "no place" but also the "*eu*-topia," or "happy place," art can perform a space of contradictions and impossibilities. Perhaps this can approximate truths about our mysterious existence that are hard, if not impossible, to convey otherwise.

Notes

1. Latin title *De consolatione philosophiae.* Most scholars agree that the Old English anonymous translator was mistakenly identified as King Alfred for centuries. Godden (2009:ix).
2. As was Thomas More's *Utopia*, Castiglione's work is full of ironies and wordplay. In 1528, seven years before Sir Thomas More was executed, the Italian Count Baldassare Castiglione published *Il Cortegiano* (*The Courtier*), which featured prominently as a conduct guide for courtiers in European courts. Its brand of Christian Platonism promoted *sprezzatura,* which means "studied nonchalance," as the best way to communicate ideals. More importantly, the ideal courtier is a poet-performer who counsels the monarch successfully, keeping in mind the monarch's biases. This advice must be expedient but only to the degree to which it serves a Christian moral good (Castiglione 2003).
3. Griswold, Rosen. See Chapter 1 by Flamm.
4. See Chapter 1 by Flamm.
5. The guardians of the state are raised to believe they were born of the Earth, and rulers may use deceptions for the benefit of their subjects. *Republic.* 459c2–d2.
6. As Stanley Rosen points out, the Platonic Ideas, according to Socrates, are themselves created by god, rendering all other iterations and manifestations—in

this sense—imitative. Yet in Plato's dialogues in the *Republic*, only the poets are accused of creating artifacts "thrice-removed," as it were, when it is unclear why Plato's conception of a Platonic Ideal is not itself a "poetic" production. Rosen (1993:7).

7. Durston (2006:92).
8. Watts (1999:xviii–xxii).
9. 1999:xxv.
10. This state of affairs is described throughout as "sick," and the Lady, using poetry and philosophy, is the healer: she says she will use gentle "medicines" before administering more powerful ones. Boethius (1999:18). This metaphorical connection is also seen in *Utopia*, where Raphael is likened to a "healer" "who wishes to heal a state which is sicker than it knows" McCutcheon (2015:30–31). Plato uses a similar analogy too: *Republic*, 425e–426a.
11. Most translations of *Utopia* do not include the poems. More (1995:19).
12. Baker-Smith "Words and Deeds," reprinted in More (2011:250,253).
13. More (2011:97).
14. More writes also writes, "Unless I had a historian's devotion to fact, I am not so stupid as to have used those barbarous and senseless names of Utopia, Anyder, Amaurot, and Ademus" (1992:124–125).
15. McCutcheon (2015:20–21).
16. More (2011:52–57).
17. Greenblatt's *Renaissance Self-Fashioning* deftly explores Thomas More's adaptability (2005).
18. More (2011:37).
19. More (2011:33–34).
20. "This purifying of wit, this enriching of memory, enabling of judgment, and enlarging of conceit, which commonly we call learning, under what name so ever it come forth, or to what immediate end soever it be directed, the final end is, to lead and draw us to as high a perfection, as our degenerate souls made worse by their clay lodgings, can be capable of" Sidney (1890:12).
21. Sidney (1890:24).
22. Sidney (1890:17).
23. Sidney (1890:eg 19).
24. "Or [what better way to fashion] a whole commonwealth, as the way of Sir Thomas More's Utopia?" Sidney (1890:17). Sidney says the "way" More created it (poetically) is better than if he had fashioned it as a philosopher would.
25. Sidney, using evidence from other Platonic dialogues, claims Plato was misunderstood and actually only wanted to weed out bad poets who would corrupt. Sidney (1890:41–42).
26. Sidney (1890:17).
27. Sidney (1595:online, np).
28. It almost certainly responds to Stephen Gosson's *School of Abuse,* which was dedicated to Sidney in 1579.
29. Sidney (1890:1–2).
30. Sidney (1890:17).
31. "[T]hus much Curse I must send you in the behalfe of all Poets:—that while you live, you live in love, and never get favor for lacking skill of a sonnet, and when you die, your memory die from the earth for want of an epitaph" Sidney (1890:58).

32. Nebrija (1996:3): "language has always been the companion of empire, following it so closely that both have always come into being, grown and flourished together, just as they have declined" (translation mine).
33. Shelley (2012:54).
34. Lamb (2018:5).
35. Unlike Adorno, Benjamin saw potential for salutary protest in pop art.
36. *Culture as Weapon* (2018).

References

Baker-Smith, Dominic. "Words and Deeds." In *Utopia*, by Thomas More, edited by George M. Logan, 241–299. New York: Norton, 2011.

Boethius, Anicius Manlius Torquatus Severinus, and Victor Ernest Watts. *The Consolation of Philosophy*. London: Penguin Books, 1999.

Boethius, Malcolm Godden, Susan Irvine, Mark Griffith, and Rohini Jayatilaka. *The Old English Boethius: An Edition of the Old English Versions of Boethiuss De Consolatione Philosophiae*. Oxford: Oxford University Press, 2009.

Castiglione, Baldassare and George Bull. *The Courtier*. London: Penguin Books, 2003.

Durston, Christopher, and Jacqueline Eales. *The Culture of English Puritanism, 1560–1700*. Basingstoke: Palgrave Macmillan, 2006.

Greenblatt, Stephen. *Renaissance Self-Fashioning: From More to Shakespeare; With a New Preface*. Chicago: University of Chicago Press, 2005.

Mccutcheon, Elizabeth. "Thomas More, Raphael Hythlodaeus, and the Angel Raphael." *Moreana* 52, Number 201 (2015): 17–36. https://doi.org/10.3366/more.2015.52.3-4.5.

More, Thomas. *Utopia*. Edited by Robert M. Adams. New York: W.W. Norton & Company, 1992.

More, Thomas. *Utopia: Latin Text and English Translation*. Edited by George Logan et al. Cambridge: Cambridge University Press, 1995.

More, Thomas. *Utopia*. Edited by George Logan. New York: W.W. Norton and Company, 2011.

Nebrija, Antonio de, and Biblioteca Serrano Morales. *Gramática Castellana*. Valencia: Vicent García Editores, 1993.

Plato, and C.D.C. Reeve. *Republic*. Indianapolis: Hackett Pub. Co., 2004.

Rosen, Stanley. *The Quarrel between Philosophy and Poetry: Studies in Ancient Thought*. New York: Routledge, 1993.

Shelley, Percy Bysshe, and J.M. Beach. *A Defense of Poetry, and Other Essays*. Austin, TX: West by Southwest Press, 2012.

Sidney, Philip. *The Defense of Poesy*. Edited by Albert S. Cook. Athenaeum Press, 1890.

Sidney, Philip, and Risa Stephanie Bear. "Defence of Poesie." Defence of Poesie (Ponsonby, 1595). Renascence Editions. Accessed March 10, 2020. www.luminarium.org/renascence-editions/defence.html#Introduction.

Thompson, Nato. *Culture as Weapon: The Art of Influence in Everyday Life*. Brooklyn, NY: Melville House, 2018.

4 La Malinche and the Noble Lie

John Burns

Language's ability or inability to make claims on truth is central to the quarrel this book has been examining. As Flamm points out it in the first chapter of this book, "the undesirable passions targeted by Plato's assault on poetry . . . ha[ve] forced Western poets into a posture of rebellion." In a similar vein, Quinn explains how the decision to speak or remain silent in certain historical circumstances, in the cases of both Vergil and Broch, is "viscerally pertinent." What happens when the artist knows that he or she is not interested in the truth but rather in the creation of a lie? How tightly can a lie become interwoven with the truth? What happens if the lie and the truth cannot be separated again? These questions are of central concern to the quarrel between poetry and philosophy, and, furthermore, inform the debates about the value of precise knowledge, the power of language and the importance of expertise central to virtually all academic disciplines today. For Plato, poetry is a form of embellishment that seeks to excite the listener and, ultimately, to dilute or pervert the truth. Some interpreters of Plato, such as Gould, emphasize that it is the licentiousness at the heart of the poesis that renders it untrustworthy. Leaving aside the fact that the attack on artistic embellishment is implicitly complicated by virtue of being written in the form of an artistically embellished dialogue, there is a moment in the *Republic* that engages the problem of lying directly. In Book III, Plato turns to the matter of the role of the noble lie in the preservation of the ideal city-state. Who has told noble lies and to what ends? Is there a good reason to do so? What is at stake when we tell a "noble lie"?

In this chapter, I will examine Plato's discussions of poetry through the lens of the Spanish Conquest of Mexico (1518–1521) in the hopes of exemplifying some of the real-world implications of the concepts that Plato put forth. In particular, I will focus on the woman who interpreted for Spanish conqueror Hernán Cortez. A woman who spoke a variety of Mayan natively, she also spoke Nahuatl, the language of the Aztecs, and later learned to speak Spanish and became the Spaniards' interpreter on their journey towards

Tenochtitlan, the seat of the Aztec empire. She is known in different cultural settings by different names: Malinalli or Malintzin in indigenous languages, doña Marina for the Spanish, and La Malinche in subsequent Mexican history. She has been represented in the chronicles of the Conquest and in more contemporary literary imaginings in such a great variety of ways that they are difficult to reconcile with a single historical personage. The variety of embellished tales that surround her develop in ways that elucidate Plato's considerations of the relationship between poetry and the ideal state.

Towards the end of Book III of the *Republic* Socrates explains the concept of the "noble lie" to Glaucon. The lie states that humankind is born of the earth, and yet everyone has different metals in their bloodstream that correspond to their station, namely bronze, silver, and gold. Simply put, this lie functions to preserve collective faith in the state as well as to justify and maintain the hierarchies within it. Plato writes:

> "Could we," I said, "somehow contrive one of those lies that come into being in case of need, of which we were just now speaking, someone noble lie to persuade, in the best case, even the rulers, but if not them, the rest of the city?"
>
> (Bloom, 1991, 93)

Later, the "case of need" is elaborated as a call to defend the city: the inhabitants of the city must "defend it, if anyone attacks, and they must think of the other citizens as brothers and born of the earth" (Bloom, 1991, 94).

Why refer to the tale of as a "lie" rather than as a "myth," as would be the case with the Myth of Er, for example? For Allan Bloom, the reasoning does not have to do with the substance of the tales but rather with their intent:

> The difference between a parable and this tale is that the man who hears a parable is conscious that it is an invention the truth of which is not in its literal expression, whereas the inhabitants of Socrates' city are to believe the untrue story to be true.
>
> (1991, 15)

Bloom goes on to note that the lie, wrapped up in the poetic shell, serves the purpose of inhibiting and controlling desire: "The noble lie is designed to give men grounds for resisting, in the name of the common good, their powerful desires" (1991, 368).

The turn towards the tightly controlled lie is referred to as medicinal in the *Republic*'s protracted metaphor of the body as polis. The lie is, in essence, political, a form of control and limitation of speech and thought in the ideal republic. Rosen summarizes the role of the guardians as being permitted to

use poetry as a beneficial lie, because they "know what they are doing" (10).
As Alessandra Aloisi and Danilo Manca note:

> If poetry and philosophy are activities that stand on the same footing,
> one may argue that Plato's thesis against art and poetry, far from dealing
> with the problem of truth and its representation, has a purely political
> meaning. By banishing poetry from the polis that is ruled according to
> philosophical principles, Plato was trying to prevent a free circulation
> of words and discourses that might divert bodies from their social and
> intellectual destination.
>
> (2015, 3)

The good which the lie defends is not disinterested and transcendent but
rather intentional and particularly located.

There is much that would be lost by mapping an ancient Greek dialogue
onto the Conquest of Mexico. Nevertheless, there are some worthwhile
points of comparison. The history of La Malinche and the multiple projections of meaning onto the relative blank screen of her existence fits squarely
into the quarrel between poetry and philosophy.

La Malinche herself is voiceless. By that I mean that written accounts
of her life are written by others, often at a great remove from her circumstances. Despite the fact that her gifts with language gave rise to her pur-
ported power and eventual fame, she left us no testimony of her own. There
is relatively little that can be indisputably stated about La Malinche. From
several sources we can cobble together a very rough sketch of a biography.
From the chronicles, we ascertain that La Malinche, who was offered to
Cortez as a gift along with another 19 slaves in Tabasco, interpreted between
her native Mayan dialect, Spanish, and Nahuatl. She aided Cortez in reach-
ing the Aztec emperor Montezuma and interpreted for the Europeans. She
had a child with Cortez whose name was Martín. She appears to have died
sometime around 1530. To go much beyond that with regard to her biography is to steer into the stuff of mere speculation. The blank space around
the known facts of her life has become a screen on which various groups
at various times have projected what they have wanted to be true about La
Malinche and, by extension, about themselves. Roughly stated, the roles
attributed to La Malinche establish the limits of the truth that can be told at
a given time under a given set of circumstances. For the chronicles of the
Conquest, she was a Christianized princess who adopted the highest values
of the conquering Spaniards. During the independence movement, we witness a shift in her representation to that of a traitor, an enabler of the Spanish.
Post-independence, in the twentieth century, she was considered the raped
mother of the Mexican people. As notions of national identity and gender

began to shift, she would become a heroine who could negotiate multiple cultures, even forging new forms of identity.

How can we interpret the lie projected onto the blank screen of La Malinche's existence? In response to Octavio Paz's mid-twentieth-century writing on La Malinche, many writers, particularly women of Mexican heritage writing north of the border, such as Gloria Anzaldúa, Cherríe Moraga, and Ana Castillo, have written compelling essays and poems that reveal and analyze the intersection of gender and ethnicity in the construction of the figure of La Malinche. I will return to those extremely important works later in this chapter, but first I would like to pull the camera lens even farther out from the scene we are describing. By doing so, we can see that the evolution of the figure of La Malinche can be situated in the shift towards secular, Enlightenment project values in the West which rendered the categories of gender and ethnicity visible in the first place. In the broadest of terms, the gradual fall of Christendom and the rise of the nation state as the political, economic, and social fabric of the West is on full display in the process of colonization and independence in the American continent. This shift in values runs parallel with a shift in representations in La Malinche: she goes from being a Christianized princess to a symbol of international conflict. In earlier texts, particularly that of Bernal Díaz del Castillo, La Malinche was the embodiment of the greatest good the Spaniards thought they conceivably could bring to the New World, namely, Christianity. As religion slowly began to cede its importance to the role of reason, and the categories of social experience came to be perceived as malleable and evidently manmade (rather than conceived of as being granted by God), the unnegotiable good that was projected on La Malinche was no longer the Christian values of forgiveness and the absolute rule of God. Instead, La Malinche came to symbolize the exploitation of the New World by the old one. Absent the role of the divine in the interpretation of the Conquest, the cruelty and injustice of the colonizing powers are stripped bare. La Malinche became a scapegoat. Depictions of her role in the Conquest in nineteenth-century history books in Mexico tended to play up her betrayal of the autonomy of the indigenous world to which she belonged. To shift the terms slightly towards the discussion of Plato from earlier in this chapter, new guardians declared their independence from the old ones. They quite literally formed a new republic with a new set of values and had to refashion the tales they told about it.

I will now turn in more detail to a series of representations in which La Malinche stands in for a transcendent good that is not up for negotiation, in the chronicles of the Conquest, in the history books of the nineteenth century and in the cultural theory of Chicana feminists in the late twentieth century. In each case, she is a forerunner of the good at stake. Initially, she is portrayed as one of the first converts to Christianity. Later, she is regarded as a cipher for Mexico's split from Spain, and her status as first convert cedes in importance to her status as first tongue, the translator and go-between who helped the Spaniards conquer the Aztec empire. Later still, her identity having become inseparable from that of Mexicans, she is viewed as a heroine by Mexican American intellectuals who are declaring their own independence from both Anglo and Mexican traditions of thought. Her status as metaphorical first mother of the mixed blood majority of the New World comes to the fore, with her ability to cross linguistic and cultural barriers at the service of the creation of new cultural identities. All three of these instances of representation of La Malinche, as distinct as they seem, have an underlying commonality: the belief that the noble lie about her is serving a greater good than an absence of a narrative history could. The narratives that depict La Malinche display, as much as anything, the belief that they are taking their readers, in Joshua Mitchell's words, from the "darkened Cave to the divine light of the Good" (2006, 46).

In Cortez's own letters back to the Spanish crown, he refers to her as "mi lengua," my tongue, and says virtually nothing else about her. His reticence may have to do with the romantic relationship between the two and the fact that Cortez was still married to another woman in Spain at the time. The contemporary chronicler, López de Gómara, recounts her being given to the Spaniards by Indians in Tabasco as well as her helping the Spaniards avoid an almost certain death in the area Cholula where she forewarned of an ambush. Bernal Díaz del Castillo, whose *True History of the Conquest of New Spain* was written decades after the fact to counterbalance López de Gómara's account, which emphasizes the role of Cortez too greatly. Díaz construes La Malinche as a noble princess worthy of a chivalrous novel, playing up her noble ancestry and her forbearance with those who wronged her in the past. *The True History of the Conquest of New Spain* was written not only to correct the errors in other accounts but also to represent the Conquest as an act that was ultimately for the good of New Spain. The representation of La Malinche Díaz's work, as Sandra Cypess Messinger has observed, borrows from tropes that equated her "with chivalric heroes from the Spanish literary tradition" (1991, 9). Beyond being of noble lineage and possessing a commitment to the cause of Conquest, La Malinche is shown to be a remarkably forgiving person despite having been sold into slavery by her own mother. In chapter 37 of the first volume, Díaz recalls an episode when she encountered her mother and brother in 1523, after the Conquest had ended:

> When Doña Marina saw they were crying, she consoled them and told them to have no fear, that when they had given her over to the men from Xicalango, they did not know what they were doing, and she forgave

them. And she gave them many jewels of gold, and clothes, and told them to return to their town, and said that God had been very gracious to her in freeing her from the worship of Idols and making her a Christian, and letting her bear a son to her lord and master, Cortez, and in marrying her to such a gentleman as Juan Jaramillo, who was now her husband, that she would rather serve her husband and Cortez than anything else in the world, and would not exchange her place to be Cacica of all the provinces in New Spain.

(1991, 69)

Rather than punishing her mother, as Díaz implies she would be justified in doing, she not only performs the Christian gesture of forgiveness but explains her Christian orientation, just in case there were any doubt. Furthermore, not content to let any Biblical resonance slip by, Díaz points out the parallels to Joseph and the Vizier in the Old Testament: "This seems to me very much like what took place between Joseph and his brothers in Egypt when they became subject to his power over the matter of the wheat" (2000, 69).

It is worth noting that Díaz imitates Biblical as well as late medieval literary tropes to depict the Conquest, a historical moment that informs narratives of modernity. As Linda Martin Alcoff reminds, the concept of modernity relies on a continuous process of inclusion and exclusion to derive its legitimacy. She writes that modernity is a

redemptive figure that justifies the unfortunate slaughters and redeems the weakened and scattered survivors of genocide and enslavement by their assimilation to a better world. In the narrative of modernity, though, there must be a "we" who are, or become, modern, constructed alongside a "they" who are not.

(2013, 61)

In the chronicles we begin to see what, I would suggest, is the repeated fate of La Malinche: the textual manipulation of her inapprehensible true circumstances to serve the purposes of the writer of the text. Her nobility, her total acceptance of Christian values, her tactical brilliance, can be read as a project of what conquering Spaniards most wanted to see in themselves. As in the case of the myth Socrates recounts to Glaucon, La Malinche as tactical-minded princess who is rescued by her contact with the Spanish, reaffirms the goals and hierarchies of the Conquest itself. Within that context, how would the conquerors define the good? It might be tempting to think of the Spanish conquistadores as exclusively money hungry, territorially driven and exceptionally cruel. The image of the Spanish explorers and conquerors in the English-speaking world is no doubt colored by *la leyenda negra*, the black legend that the British spread about Spain as propaganda starting in the sixteenth century. However, the motives of the arriving Spaniards were probably not as exclusively materialistic as we might imagine, or at least not in terms of wealth as we would understand them today. They may well have viewed their material gain as a means towards a higher end. For example, in Todorov's reading of Christopher Columbus's diaries, he points out that Columbus's desire for gold was inseparable from his desire to serve his God. The gold from the New World, Columbus repeatedly wrote in his diaries, would serve to fund the campaigns to retake the Holy Land much as Christians had reconquered Muslim Spain in recent centuries. Todorov writes:

> The universal victory of Christianity—this is the motive that animates Columbus, a profoundly pious man (he never sets sail on Sunday), who for this very reason regards himself as chosen, as charged with a divine mission, and who sees divine intervention eve here, in the movement of the waves as in the wreck of his ship (on a Christmas night!): "By many signal miracles God has shown Himself on the voyage."
>
> (1992, 10)

God and gold in the process of Conquest, far from being categories at odds with one another, were two sides of the same evangelizing coin.

While Bernal Díaz's version of La Malinche is very different from later iterations, it shares the emphasis on intentionality in her actions. The aspiration of the late nineteenth century educational system in Mexico was to create a modern, enlightened education that rejected the barbarities of the Spanish, *la leyenda negra*, in part by praising and idealizing the pre-Hispanic past. La Malinche became the Benedict Arnold of Mexican history textbooks, the weak link in the glorious pre-Hispanic past that let the conquerors defeat the Aztec empire. To this day, in common speech, the term "malinchista," which is derived from her name, means in the Mexican context someone who betrays his or her national identity in favor of what is foreign.

Nineteenth-century Mexico, after its independence in 1821, witnessed a struggle towards modernity in which the rhetoric of scientific knowledge, progress, and reason was held up as antidotes to the evils of the colonial period. Political instabilities in the decades after independence included the rule of Santa Anna which saw Mexico lose nearly half its territory and the occupation of the country by Maximilian of Habsburg, a descendent of the same royal family that ruled Spain at the time of Cortez's Conquest of Mexico. Nonetheless, the latter part of the nineteenth century saw the return of President Benito Juárez and his liberal reforms. Educational reform in

Mexico was undertaken as a means of modernizing the nation and establishing its distinct character through nationalist discourse. The clearest record of the shift in the representation in La Malinche can be found in the history textbooks that were written and used in the course of this educational reform. Under the direction of Gabino Barreda, a physician and student of positivist philosophy appointed by President Juárez, the restructuring of the educational system was a part of a larger push towards secularization. As Jonathan Corr writes:

> Barreda became part of the national debate on structuring education by offering the values of Comtean positivism in his "Civic Oration." Mexico's historical process, he argued, involved "mental emancipation," that is, "religious," "scientific," and "political" emancipation that had finally brought down the colonial order.
>
> (2014, 101)

What role does La Malinche play in the textbooks that informed the secularizing narrative of the nation? Broadly, the pre-Hispanic past was glorified, considered a homogeneous and harmonious antidote to foreign powers that were now viewed as aggressors towards Mexico: Spain during the colonial period, the U.S. during the Mexican American War, and, most recently, France during its occupation of Mexico. In part, historians would lean heavily on the work of Bernal Díaz del Castillo, which describes the Aztec capital in terms of fantastic literature of the time, to elaborate this nationalist discourse, albeit with some important alterations. As Spanish historian Cristina González notes, La Malinche's decision to help the conquerors is emphasized. This moment, González writes:

> which Bernal Díaz adorns with all sorts of excessive details, constitutes an important moment in the historiography of the Conquest. The justification of the massacre in the Spanish sources and the praise for the behavior of Marina for having saved the conquerors' lives makes it turn out to be not so strange that the most vehement nationalist and anti-Spanish to base their work on these sources to denigrate the interpreter and that this event led to her fame as an archetypal sellout to her country.
>
> (2002, 95)

González goes on to note that the historians of the time pushed the idea that La Malinche did not warn Cortez of a possible ambush in Cholula but rather that the conspiracy to kill was "her invention" (2002, 95).

The noble lie was the invention of an ill-intentioned Malinche, a scapegoat to explain the collapse of the mighty and glorious pre-Hispanic past. This representation of La Malinche continues into the twentieth century and is featured prominently in the work of Nobel Prize winner Octavio Paz, particularly in his influential book of essays titled *The Labyrinth of Solitude*. *The Labyrinth of Solitude* is a lengthy and somewhat dated treatise on what it means to be Mexican. It includes descriptions of Mexican festivities, characteristics, and history that would seem to be fairly reductive and essentialist to a contemporary reader. Paz codifies the twentieth-century representation of La Malinche as the metaphorical mother of the Mexican nation who is, at once, both victim and traitor. He writes the following of the national grito or cry for independence celebrated on September 15: "*¡Viva México, hijos de la chingada!*" (Long live Mexico, sons of the screwed woman). Paz continues:

> If the *Chingada* is representation of the violated Mother, it is appropriate to associate her with the Conquest, which is also a violation, not only in the historical sense, but also in the very flesh of Indian women.
>
> (2002, 25)

La Malinche assumes dimensions beyond her historical identity and represents an instance of a foreign violation of the national territory.

Paz's mid-century essay would spark a conversation about the less obvious positive aspects of La Malinche among Mexican-American feminists in the subsequent decades. Reacting to Paz's clear articulation of La Malinche as violated woman, several Mexican-American feminists in the 1980s located their disenfranchisement in the space of La Malinche's erased biography, and they reimagined her as a heroine rather than as a traitor. The most well-known figure to explore the figure of La Malinche at that time was Mexican American feminist theorist Gloria Anzaldúa. She refers to La Malinche's split identity, divided between the tongues of the old world and the new, in *Borderlands/ La frontera*, a classic on Chicana identity. As a woman born between cultures and languages, Anzaldúa attempts to recognize the pain of her sense of not belonging to either but also attempts to define that cultural intersection not as an absence, as Paz would have it (not simply as a not belonging), but as a presence in the figure of the "new mestiza." Anzaldúa writes of La Malinche:

> The dark-skinned woman has been silenced, gagged, caged, bound into servitude by marriage for 300 years. . . . [She fights] for her own skin and a piece of ground to stand on, a ground from which to view the world, a perspective.
>
> (1987, 22–23)

The casting of La Malinche in a positive or negative light, or in Platonic terms, in a noble lie, serves to forge national or ethnic identities in determined historical moments: the moment when the Spanish become emphatically a "them," those other people; the moment when Mexican Independence forced a reconsideration of national identity; the moment when Chicana feminists needed to articulate their differences and their commonalities. La Malinche is a shifting mirror of the needs of radically different moments rather than a reflection of any of her actual lived experience. I would venture to say that contemporary creators of La Malinche's story are well aware that La Malinche is more of an invented figure than a historical one. Most of us know there is a dose of fiction in our history. Even Socrates, describing the "noble lie" to Glaucon, concedes that some poetry, some shiny flashes of bronze, silver, and gold, will always find its way into our philosophies.

References

Alcoff, Linda Martín. 2013. "Philosophy, the Conquest, and the Meaning of Modernity a Commentary on 'Anti-Cartesian Meditations: On the Origin of the Philosophical Anti-Discourse of Modernity' by Enrique Dussel." *Human Architecture: Journal of the Sociology of Self-Knowledge* 11:I, 57–66.

Aloisi, Alessandra and Manca, Danilo. 2015. "Introduction: The Quarrel between Poetry and Philosophy." *Odradek: Studies in Philosophy of Literature, Aesthetics and New Media Theories* I:2, 7–14.

Anzaldúa, Gloria. 1987. *Borderlands/La Frontera: The New Mestiza*. San Francisco: Aunt Lute Books.

Bloom, Allan. 1991. *The Republic of Plato*. Translated with Notes and an Interpretive Essay. New York: Basic Books

Corr, John. 2014. "The Enlightenment Surfaces in Nineteenth-Century Mexico: Scientific Thinking Attempts to Deliver Order and Progress." *History of Science* 52:10, 98–123.

Díaz del Castillo, Bernal. 2000. "From *The True History of the Conquest of New Spain*." In *Victors and Vanquished: Spanish and Nahua Views of the Conquest of Mexico*. Ed. Stuart B. Schwartz. Boston: Bedford/St. Martin's. 43–74.

González, Cristina. 2002. *Doña Marina (La Malinche) y la formación de la identidad mejicana*. Madrid: Ediciones Encuentro.

Gould, Thomas. 1990. *The Ancient Quarrel Between Poetry and Philosophy*. Princeton: Princeton UP.

Messinger, Sandra Cypess. 1991. *La Malinche In Mexican Literature from History to Myth*. Austin: University of Texas Press.

Mitchell, Joshua. 2006. *Plato's Fable Book: On the Mortal Condition in Shadowy Times*. Princeton: Princeton UP.

Paz, Octavio. 2002. "The Sons of La Malinche." In *The Mexico Reader*. Ed. Gilbert Joseph and Timothy Henderson. Durham: Duke UP. 21–27

Todorov, Tzvetan. 1992. *The Conquest of America: The Question of the Other*. New York: HarperPerennial.

5 Making and Discovering in Shakespeare's Sonnets

William Gahan

This volume concerns Plato's pronouncement from the *Republic* that poets "lie" and with ways subsequent writers have responded. As seen in Chapter 3, Sir Philip Sidney contends directly with Plato in *The Defense of Poesy* (1595), saying that his ousting of the poets in the *Republic* was misunderstood. Sidney proclaims, and Thomas More's *Utopia* (1516) suggests, that poetry allows a more open channel for truth because it provides readers and hearers with what "should be," giving salutary examples for imitation by readers, helping them improve themselves and the world.[1]

The present chapter discusses Shakespeare's 1609 sonnets and their methods of delivery in light of the quarrel between poetry and philosophy.[2] The sequence performs what Sidney and More suggest that poetry can achieve: although language is limited, it is all we have, and only imaginative creation can conceive of a permanent ideal (a "fixed mark"). However, the sequence does not attempt to ennoble the reader, as Sidney and More suggest for poetry. Shakespeare conjures Platonic ideals poetically, but he upends every attempt to follow them through absolutely, and the sequence enacts a process of continual making, discovering, and failing. He deploys literary and philosophical modes of inquiry through this "making" and "discovering," as will be discussed later in this chapter. That the ideals proposed in the sonnets fail in the face of human and linguistic limitations shows that they were always poetically-conceived ideals—not attainable truths—and this suggests that Plato's ideas as conceived in the *Republic* partake of poetic creation too. Rather than ennoble, the sonnets effectuate a rhetorical display of skill (through the human drama of a lover's inconsistent attempts to control his feelings and those of others) that may outlast competitors, conferring a legacy on the memory of the poet and his love.

In Shakespeare's sonnets, the question of whether poetry makes a positive contribution to "truth" seems different from that question in the *Republic*. This is mostly because the poems are about love and its emotional, social, and psychological effects, and not about how to fashion an ideal society, which was Plato's aim in the *Republic*. Pondering the sonnets' aesthetic use of Platonic ideas may help clarify Plato's differing purposes in the *Republic* versus the *Symposium*.

In contrast to what he says about poetry in the *Republic*, Plato's discussion of love in the *Symposium*, so largely dependent upon desire and emotion, unapologetically partakes of both literary and philosophical expression. In the *Republic*, the poets are ousted for lying but the guardians of the state can be raised on salutary lies as if this were not a vexed position. Here, Plato does not trust the literary mode of "making" because emotional responses—rather than rational ones—may lead hearers astray from Plato's poetic vision of a political ideal. In *Symposium*, this issue seems less of a problem because Plato's ideal is of love. But even in *Symposium*, as David Fuller notes, there is a "clash of . . . philosophical and literary ways of reading." For the philosophical mode, "there is finally truth; the purpose of interpretation is to elicit truth." For the literary mode, "different truths are embedded in an undecidable contest of perspectives; the purpose of interpretation is to elicit embeddedness, context, and relationships. *Symposium* is as much literary as philosophical: undecidability is implicit in its mode."[3] Still, the context of all the dialogues is literary. Questions conjure responses and further questions; there are jokes, puns, and the moving in and out of the subject of inquiry to the circumstances and characters considering them. Discoveries arise as the characters create metaphors, hypotheticals, and analogies towards further questions and answers. As Fuller puts it, "Socrates is a character in a historical fiction."

Shakespeare's sonnets surely perform both modes of inquiry that Rosen and Griswold call "making" (literary, artistic) versus "discovering" (philosophical).[4] Plato was moving amid different modes in each dialogue as well, and he did not always privilege "discovering." Before discussing how the sonnets enact the process of "making" and "discovering, an overview is in order, beginning with their reception.

The sonnets had a dramatic reception ever since their 1609 publication in London along with "A Lover's Complaint."[5] John Benson's 1640 edition removed this last poem and changed some references to the love object of the male speaker from "he" to "she." Edmund Malone's 1790 text restored the original 1609 text with "A Lover's Complaint." The English Romantics in the nineteenth century "rediscovered" them, although not without trepidation regarding expressions of love from a man for another man. The addressee of Tennyson's "In Memoriam," Henry Hallam, wished they had "never been written,"[6] perhaps due to homoerotic content. Much modern criticism of the sonnets approaches them as a sequence, sometimes with "A Lover's Complaint" and sometimes without.[7]

However, as with so many things said about them, the internal evidence of the sonnets themselves does not seal with absolute certainty the traditionally accepted separation of the sonnets addressed to the young man (1–126) and those addressed to the "dark lady" (127–152). Critics disagree on whether they are biographical, completely fictional, or somewhere in between. Until relatively recently, equal disagreement existed about whether the poet's addresses to the young man were un-erotic or whether they were homosexual, which is now the popular view.[8] In any case, by way of varying conventions to be expected in early modern English poetry, the sonnets do conjure a sense of interiority through the interplay of desire and emotion that is never satisfactorily resolved. Any truth they express is achieved via a rhetorical performance of tumultuous love, with the powerful and contradictory emotions attempting to resolve themselves—and failing.

Given this, a contested but traditionally popular narrative for the sonnets could be described as follows:[9] a poet-lover, the speaker, tries to convince a "lovely boy" to have a child with a woman in order to pass on his beauty before he dies; the sonnets then take a turn in preference for the speaker's verse to memorialize the young man. The poet is disheartened at various points about unchaste behavior by the young man, whom he defends, even while chastising him. He also feels competitive about other poets who praise him. The young man is figured as a Platonic pattern of perfect beauty. After admitting that time will eventually catch up with and destroy his love (the young man), the poet turns to poems about his own mistress (the "dark lady"), with whom it seems the young man has also had sex. These sonnets are more carnal, and the sequence ends with two mythological sonnets about Cupid and references to venereal disease, wherein love conquers all.[10] As will be discussed later, if we include "The Lover's Complaint," originally published with the sonnets in the 1609 edition, as part of the narrative, then the young man in this poem may be the one from the sonnets;[11] here, a crying confession from a betrayed woman rebukes him.[12]

Turning to some of the sonnets' methods of delivery, we see that NeoPlatonism was only one available channel through which early modern writers navigated. NeoPlatonism aims to transcend sensual love through the apprehension of beauty in order to achieve spiritual integrity.[13] The sonnets depict Platonic and NeoPlatonic patterns of thought, but they are not successfully carried out, nor are they supposed to be.[14] Rather, the speaker uses these conventions to express his desires, but he does not consistently expect the sonnets to achieve what NeoPlatonism tries to achieve. The narrative from Diotima in *Symposium* illustrates what NeoPlatonism is "supposed to achieve."

Several critics have pointed out that Shakespeare's sonnets recall Diotima's approach to love.[15] She describes a vision of universal love kindled from particular loves, culminating in a direct perception of "the beauty the lover has so long toiled for." Socrates was so convinced by this that he wanted to spread the good news, declaring that everyone "should worship the god of Love."[16] David Fuller writes that for Plato, love is an essential force of the universe and the proper conduit towards philosophy, the love of wisdom. However, not every kind of love achieves wisdom: "Love governed by common Aphrodite is concerned with sex [and] is directed towards men or women. Love governed by heavenly Aphrodite is concerned with . . . beauty, intelligence, and moral worth; it is directed exclusively toward men."[17] Long have similar observations been ascribed to the poet's love for the "Dark Lady" (Sexual) versus that for the young man (Ideal/Platonic), but a close reading of the sonnets does not uphold this neatly.

This is because the speaker loves the young man sexually as well, and there are instances in which he enjoins the dark lady to use her art to uphold ideals. Rafael Koskimies states that the effect of the sonnets is "first and foremost based on the gradual approach to the ideal of beauty and love so explicitly stated by Diotima . . . in the *Symposium*."[18] However, the sonnets do not achieve the ethereal integrity Diotima's vision suggests, nor does the poet-speaker seem to expect them to: the sonnets end with a joke about the unquenchable nature of love and with a suggestion of venereal disease.

In addition to appropriating conventions creatively, the performance also partakes of authorial distancing common in the early modern period. As did Petrarch and Dante in their sequences, and More in his *Utopia*, each in their own way, Shakespeare sometimes projects himself into the speaker and sometimes steps away without ever proffering an unequivocal revelation.[19] The emotions and treacheries in the sonnets are woven among various love interests; there is a deflection of authorial self amid furtive looks cloaked in convention—and all of this tells truths about the complicated workings of lust, love, and the desire to avoid shame. Building anew and failing again works like a cycle, ultimately leaving its readers befuddled, denied absolute closure. There is a "truth" that arises from this, as I will suggest later.

To illustrate how "making" and "discovering" help turn the cycle, let us begin with the first few sonnets. The procreation sonnets, 1–17, in which the young man is enjoined to reproduce, also reflect Diotima's ideas that "procreation is the nearest thing to perpetuity and immortality" and that "Love is love of immortality as well as the good."[20] In Sonnet 11, the young man is told that nature "carv'd thee for her seale," and he should "print more, not let that coppy die." As if to test this idea through the making of the poem, discoveries ensue along the way. Unlike the sequences by Petrarch, in which transcendence seems sought more earnestly and consistently through desire towards a heavenly kind of love, if often with irony and admission of failure, sonnets in Shakespeare's sequence celebrate a performance of often contrary convictions.[21] Discoveries along the way find poetically permanent rooms (*stanzas*), only to be contradicted in the next sonnet with a newly-made discovery. For example, consider Sonnet 17:

> Who will believe my verse in time to come,
> If it were filled with your most high deserts?
> Though yet heaven knows it is but as a tomb
> Which hides your life and shows not half your parts:
> If I could write the beauty of your eyes,
> And in fresh numbers number all your graces,
> The age to come would say this Poet lies,
> Such heavenly touches ne'er touch'd earthly faces.
> So should my papers (yellowed with their age)
> Be scorn'd, like old men of less truth than tongue,
> And your true rights be term'd a Poet's rage,
> And stretched metre of an Antique song.
> But were some child of yours alive that time,
> You should live twice in it, and in my rhyme.

Here, the speaker aligns poetry with the charges leveled against it in Plato's *Republic*: it is but a poet's rage, and it stretches the truth. The couplet, however, communicates a new discovery. Now the speaker affirms that if the young man has a child, the poet's truth will be verified, lending life to the rhyme. In the *Symposium*, it is important to Plato that the "word" be internalized in the emotions and realities of the listener. Poetically, the symbol must connect with its reality.[22] In this poem, the truth of the young man's beauty seeks a physical vehicle through progeny that vouches for the words of the sonnets: the flesh substantiates the word anew in times to come. But even here, poetic truth is dependent upon the life of a descendant. The next sonnet (18) famously explodes into a brazen affirmation of the sole power of poetry:

> Shall I compare thee to a Summer's day?

In 18, the speaker now wields the pen confidently as an instrument of creation. The young man is likened to an ideal of "fair." That "every fair from fair sometime declines" enacts the difficulty in knowing the difference between an image and its original: the line can be confusing because both "fair" (the individual instance) and "fair" (the ideal) look exactly the same in the poem. The speaker affirms that the young man's "eternal summer shall not fade," and his ideal form shall never wander in death's shade. He says, "in eternal lines to time thou growest." Not only will the "lines" of descendants further his name, but the poetic lines will partake of eternity. The final couplet famously reads, "So long as men can breathe or eyes can see, / So long lives this, and this gives life to thee."

This testament to the power of poetry rings loudly, as if the speaker were experiencing a wonderful discovery. It is surely a step beyond the timid gestures seen in Sonnet 15, in which the speaker artistically "grafts" the young man's virtues against the ravages of time. The sonnet enacts in two instances what Sir Philip Sidney says poetry can do: it creates a "new nature," in one sense with a young man who is not subject to decay, and in another in its ability to create legacies, giving life to the young man's beauty through poetry.[23] Sonnet 19 yields anew to time's destructive nature, but then summons this: "Yet do thy worst, old Time, despite thy wrong, / My love shall in my verse ever live young." These sonnets about time ebb and flow between affirming their power to memorialize and lamenting destruction, like the waves of generations in Sonnet 60 that "contend" in "sequent toil" towards the inevitable shore.

In 53, the speaker fashions the young man as archetype of all nature: "What is your substance, whereof are you made, / That millions of strange shadows on you tend?" The love object is made perfect in the eyes of the lover, imagined as generative of all nature, a powerful muse for the expression of true feelings. It closes thus: "In all external grace you have some part, / But you like none, none you, for constant heart." Many lovers sense that love abides all, and the sonnets express this intimation of immortality. The older speaker enacts his erotic and intellectual love for the young man through a performance that reflects Diotoma's narrative,[24] seeking to affix an ideal, but only as an impulse in the moment that yields to doubt (sometimes based on the young man's behavior)—and then rekindles his hopes anew.

As shown earlier, the poet frequently fashions the young man as the bright sun of a Platonic ideal (whose cheating is forgiven). The dark lady, who appears in the latter portion, is often (though not always) described as deceitful.[25] Joel Fineman sees the poet as losing admiration for the young man, but still feeling love and lust for him, which spins him into a confusion of emotional and sexual experiences with the "dark lady."[26] However, although the speaker often covers for the youth, he also chastises him and the lady for cheating on him (the speaker). Even the poet seems to admit to infidelity, both sexually and in his poetry (151, 152). So whether or not, as Dubrow claims, some sonnets critics think are about the dark lady are actually about the young man or another lover, the fact remains that betrayal and shame are felt; a strong desire for integrity is felt; and disappointment in others and in the self is continually assuaged with creative affirmations of love and integrity.[27] Perhaps ironically in light of the quarrel between poetry and philosophy, it is the *poetic* affirmations that shoot for "truth" while the "realistic" "discoveries" belie the duplicity of human behavior. To approximate "truth" then, both creating and discovering are needed.

In "A Lover's Complaint," the poem that appears immediately after the sonnets in the original publication, other voices enter the drama: a female lover expresses forlorn grief caused by a young man who is made to look shameful. If we accept this poem as completing the sequence, then the once-ideal young man's shame is now finally exposed—after the speaker felt it for himself and ascribed it to the "dark lady."[28] Attempts at affixing narratives to the sequence are salutary, but strict adherence to them is misguided: the sonnets partake in the plenitude of Shakespearean creation and are resilient place-holders for various suggestive interpretations.

Still, the sonnets clarify the poet's will to honor an ever-fixed mark, creating a poetic desire for permanence in a fleeting and treacherous world. Sonnet 116 is the most famous example from the sequence of a vision of Platonic-like permanence. The poem can be read cynically at one extreme or sentimentally at another. This reinforces both the limits of language in conveying a vision of perfection—as well as poetry's sovereign power to conjure such a vision at all.

> Let me not to the marriage of true minds
> Admit impediments. Love is not love
> Which alters when it alteration finds,
> Or bends with the remover to remove:
> O no; it is an ever fixed mark,
> That looks on tempests, and is never shaken;
> It is the star to every wandering bark,
> Whose worth's unknown, although his height be taken.
> Love's not Time's fool, though rosy lips and cheeks
> Within his bending sickle's compass come;
> Love alters not with his brief hours and weeks,
> But bears it out even to the edge of doom.
> If this be error and upon me proved,
> I never writ, nor no man ever loved.

Before addressing the poem, let us recall the love vision of Diotima from the *Symposium*. Ronald Gray says the sonnet poet "adopts this ideal love as his own. But he does not speak of any long pilgrimage such as Diotima describes, and may have simply adopted her description as satisfying his ambition."[29] In 116, this overwhelming love is felt as stronger than death. With its Christian and Platonic echoes, it easily conveys a desire for unity and permanence. But it describes an eternal, fixed ideal for love that is not humanly possible. This "love is not love." Marina Marin comments on a similar impossibility regarding the conclusion of Diotima's speech: "the proposed contemplation is not fit for human beings . . . because . . . the unstated assumption on Diotima's part . . . suggests that a wholly disembodied contemplation can be combined with the embodied life of a human being. That is impossible."[30] Diotima's vision of disembodied love is all-poetic, all ideal, but a fully "truthful" expression of desire for the Socrates of the *Symposium*, even if it is impossible for a flesh-and-blood human to achieve it.

Yes, the poem invites ironic interpretations. Must human love never change? Can it never grow, learn, or flower? The play of negatives in the couplet also belie the skeptical reactions of a speaker who is unsure of himself. These are ways the sonnets show the inconsistent workings of the speaker's mind. Again, more examples are found in his desire for the young man to symbolize the Good, his willingness to use art to cover the young man's defects, and his quickness to blame the woman for transgressions he had heretofore forgiven from the young man. In all, we see a performance of an imperfect soul armed with visions of integrity but fueled by desire and thwarted by mutability and the diseased nature of impermanent and treacherous love. The sonnets perform, over and again, a cycle of desire and failed attempts to transcend it.

There is a deep truth to this poetic method. It conveys feelings as they may actually affect human beings: in contradictory and complicated ways. Emotions and reason interact to convey inner experiences. Of course, the artist makes and discovers these emotions, inspired by the thoughts and experiences of love and life to fashion poetry. Peter Lamarque intriguingly applies the sonnets to the philosopher R.G. Collingwood's theory of aesthetic conveyance of feelings, which happens through a process that gives them shape. As discussed previously, the sonnets weave art and procreation in order to fight the ravages of time to preserve the young man. Lamarque asserts, as boldly as does the speaker of the sonnets, that the poems bring to being the eternity of love: "it is not a mere contingency—a matter of hope or aspiration—that the love will survive as long as the sonnets survive. It is now shown to be a *necessary* truth." Lamarque refers to the aesthetic creation and discovery of a love inspired by the young man's beauty, not any particular description of it: "This after all is not something that Time can destroy" because a poem is not "identical to any physical description of it."[31] Lamarque is aware that even if this were true, its eternal nature can only be tested, as Sonnet 18 knows, "as long as men can breathe, or eyes can see."

For me, the sonnets do not attempt to achieve transcendent love as Diotima describes it—nor as Lamarque describes it either. Lamarque makes a good point that a vision of love for the young man still exists today through the poems. But the uninscribed, eternal *idea* of a poem he conjures is like the (impossible) Platonic, "ever fixed mark" dubiously affirmed in Sonnet 116.

The Platonic vision of the "fixed mark" is poetic, invisible, and in many ways, "untrue." Not only was love in *Symposium* conjured poetically, but Plato's ideal society in the *Republic* was too. It is at least as dependent upon "making" as upon "discovering" for its existence. Shakespearean evocations of poetic and philosophical truths evince an impatience with the limits of language (the famous Sonnet 130 mocks poetic comparisons), but they embrace language anyway. In his works, both art (making) and philosophy (discovering) pay homage to lived experience: Their truth lies in the interplay of contrarieties and ambitions that gain traction and then flag, conveying an overall picture of the ways the vagaries of love, lust, hope, and disappointment may actually play out in life.

In the *Republic*, Plato wanted to kick out the poets to preserve the ennobling nature of his own poetic vision. The sonnets perform truths about emotions and troubled relationships, but they do not conform to Sir Philip Sidney's argument that poetry "ennobles" through examples for emulation.[32] In the nineteenth century, English poets Charles and Mary Lamb published *Tales from Shakespeare*, in which they claim strongly that Shakespearean drama instructed and ennobled young readers, preparing them for the lessons of the plays as they get older. The Lamb's silence about the sonnets lends credence to the idea that even in a milieu sympathetic to the salutary influences of literature, they did not stand out for this effect.[33] Although modern readers may find some sonnets inspiring (116 is often recited at weddings), few would claim they strive to impart a moral effect.

As cited by Stephanie Quinn in this volume, Theodor Adorno said that after Auschwitz, poetry was "barbaric."[34] The failure of the Enlightenment showed that humanity will always contend with its own savage nature, its diseased loves, and its treacherous and animalistic impulses. Poetry too will always be another act of savagery, imperfectly expressing all of these truths, displaying a savage dance of Apollo and Dionysius. The ennobling and also corrupting influences of deep emotions will exist "as long as eyes can see and men can breathe," and any totalizing conception of how to harness them for philosophical or moral purposes will forever be susceptible to ongoing destruction and revision. That is, it is up to the reader. Reading about a lover with intense emotions trying to control his own and others' behavior does not seem ennobling, at least not in a didactic way. Rather, as Pope Francis writes, it may remind us that we are all "a complex mixture of lights and shadows."[35]

Notes

1. Sidney (1890:22). See also Chapter 3, note 22.
2. I use the 1609 sonnets with my own spelling and punctuation emendations for clarity.

3. Fuller (2011:25). Compare also Flamm's discussion of Plato's *Phaedrus* in Chapter 1.
4. See Chapter 1.
5. Fineman's *Perjured Eye* argues that the narrative of the sequence imparts a novel literary persona through a rhetorical display of skill, which, as many have pointed out, is a common competitive purpose for early modern writers. There are some Shakespearean sonnets that explicitly contend with a rival poet's poetic prowess.
6. Matz (2008:186).
7. Kerrigan's (1986) and Duncan-Jones's (1998) editions restore the "Complaint." Jane Kingsley-Smith calls for a study of the reception of the individual sonnets, rather than the *Sonnets* (as a narrative), because most readers know them as individual lyrics, free from assumptions about any narrative context within which they "should" be interpreted. Kingsley-Smith (2019:4). In this chapter, the sonnets are approached as a sequence.
8. Fuller and many others point out that Platonic, idealized love, inspired by beauty, as seen in the *Symposium* and the *Phaedrus*, is understood to be felt erotically by an older man for boy (2011:28).
9. Viewing them only as a narrative is also contested. For example, Heather Dubrow, in "Incertainties now crown themselves assur'd," posits that they may be independent, "internalized meditations" in the lyric mode Schiffer (2000:123).
10. Burrow suggests a fifth century passage by Marianus Scholasticus as a possible source for 153 and 154 (2002:117).
11. Ilona Bell, in "That Which Thou Hast Done," notes this possibility. Schiffer (2000:455–474).
12. Gray, citing Kerrigan (1986) and Duncan-Jones (1997), points out it was common in Shakespeare's day to publish sonnet sequences along with a coda like "The Lover's Complaint" (2011:65).
13. NeoPlatonism was Platonism as appropriated by writers like Pietro Bembo and Baldassare Castiglione.
14. Gray (2011:1–4; 10–16). Gray joins many others in pointing out Christian references too.
15. Fuller (2011:23–24); Gray, (2011: 3–10,23).
16. *The Symposium*, p. 211, Qt. by Gray (2010:3).
17. Fuller (2011:22).
18. Koskimies (1970:270).
19. Kerrigan sees it this way: "The text is neither fictive nor confessional. Shakespeare stands behind the first person of his sequence as Sidney had stood behind Astrophil—sometimes near the poetic 'I,' sometimes farther off, but never without some degree of rhetorical projection" (1986:11).
20. *Symposium*, Qt. by Koskimies (1970:267).
21. Gray discusses Shakespearean opposites: "His mind would seem to be always straddling them both, never committed to one or the other and yet totally committed to both: he loves totally and mocks or denies totally" (2011:24).
22. Fuller (2011:28).
23. Sidney (1890:7). Other than the initials "W.H.," the name of the young man is withheld.
24. Gray, Fuller, Koskimies.
25. In many of the dark lady sonnets, enduring visions of love are upended by the trappings of desire. As in 138, the speaker encourages the lady to use her arts

to uphold his ideal image of love. In the sonnets directed to the young man, the speaker's resources of art are sufficient to affirm the ideal despite the youth's behavior (e.g., Sonnets 58 and 88).
26. Fineman (1986:55).
27. Dubrow, in "Incertainties now crown themselves assur'd" Schiffer (2000:118: 113–154).
28. Ilona Bell, who conjectures the young man of "A Lover's Complaint" may be the young man of the sonnets, makes this point very convincingly in "That which thou hast done," in which she also argues that the private personae of the sequence and final poem have been adapted as a public personae for publication, and that the shame ascribed to various players in the sonnets is protected by withholding names and other narrative devices. Schiffer (2000:455–474).
29. Gray (2011:7).
30. Marren. Reid (2019:138).
31. "Beauty and Time in the Sonnets." Bourne (2019:534–535).
32. See Chapter 3.
33. Lamb (2018:5).
34. See Chapter 6.
35. Pope Francis (2016:86).

References

Bell, Ilona. "'That Which Thou Hast Done': Shakespeare's Sonnets and A Lover's Complaint." In *Shakespeare's Sonnets: Critical Essays*, edited by James Schiffer, 455–474. New York: Garland Publishing, 2000.

Bourne, Craig, and Emily Caddick Bourne. *The Routledge Companion to Shakespeare and Philosophy*. London: Routledge, an imprint of the Taylor & Francis Group, 2019.

Burrow, Colin. *Shakespeare: The Complete Sonnets and Poems*. Oxford: Oxford University Press, 2002.

Dubrow, Heather. "Incertainties Now Crown Themselves Assur'd: The Politics of Plotting Shakespeare's Sonnets." In *Shakespeare's Sonnets: Critical Essays*, edited by James Schiffer, 113–134. New York: Garland Publishing, 2000.

Fineman, Joel. *Shakespeare's Perjured Eye: The Invention of Poetic Subjectivity in the Sonnets*. Berkeley: University of California Press, 1986.

Francis, Pope. *Amoris Laetitia: the Joy of Love*. Word Among Us Press, 2016.

Fuller, David. *The Life in the Sonnets*. London: Continuum, 2011.

Gray, Ronald D. *Shakespeare on Love: the Sonnets and Plays in Relation to Plato's Symposium, Alchemy, Christianity and Renaissance Neo-Platonism*. Newcastle: Cambridge Scholars, 2011.

Kingsley-Smith, Jane. *The Afterlife of Shakespeare's Sonnets*. Cambridge: Cambridge University Press, 2019.

Koskimies, Rafael. "The Question of Platonism in Shakespeare's Sonnets." *Neuphilologische Mitteilungen* 71, 1970, 260–270.

Lamarque, Peter. "Beauty and Time in the Sonnets." In *The Routledge Companion to Shakespeare and Philosophy*, edited by Craig Bourne and Emily Caddick Bourne, 525–540. New York: Routledge, 2019.

Lamb, Charles, and Mary Lamb. *Tales From Shakespeare*. New York: Sterling, 2018.

Marren, Marina. "Ascent to the Αὐτὸ Τὸ Καλόν in Plato's Symposium 204a–212d." In *Looking at Beauty to Kalon in Western Greece: Selected Essays from the 2018 Symposium on the Heritage of Western Greece*, edited by Heather Reid, 133–148. Sioux City, IA: Parnasus Press, 2019.

Matz, Robert. *The World of Shakespeare's Sonnets: An Introduction*. Jefferson, NC: McFarland, 2008.

Plato, and C.D.C. Reeve. *Republic*. Indianapolis, IN: Hackett Pub. Co., 2004.

Plato, and Robin Waterfield. *Symposium*. Oxford: Oxford University Press, 2008.

Rosen, Stanley. *The Quarrel between Philosophy and Poetry: Studies in Ancient Thought*. New York: Routledge, 1993.

Schiffer, James. *Shakespeare's Sonnets: Critical Essays*. New York: Garland Publishing, 2000.

Shakespeare, William. *Shakespeare's Sonnets Being a Reproduction in Facsimile of the First Edition, 1609, from the Copy in the Malone Collection in the Bodleian Library*. Edited by Sidney Lee. Los Angeles, CA: University of California Libraries, 1905.

Shakespeare, William, and John Kerrigan. *The Sonnets: And, A Lovers Complaint/ William Shakespeare*. Harmondsworth: Penguin, 1986.

Shakespeare, William, and Katherine Duncan-Jones. *Shakespeare's Sonnets*. London: Thomson Learning, 1998.

Sidney, Philip. *The Defense of Poesy*. Edited by Albert S. Cook. Boston, MA: Athenaeum Press, 1890.

6 Vergil, Broch, and a "Place" for Art

Answering the Quarrel

Stephanie Quinn

As I showed in my previous chapter of this volume, the histories of the first century BCE and the early twentieth century CE run parallel in manifold particulars of their upside down realities; in the shared perceptions of their times as pivotal; in looking to the deep past to clarify, ratify, or critique the present for the sake of some projected future. Some contemporaries in these millennial moments asked how artists might devise art that speaks true when truth itself does not seem real or even possible. In this chapter, I analyze the artistic responses of the ancient Roman epic poet Vergil and the modern Austrian novelist Hermann Broch.

Art and Lies

In addition to his novels, Broch left essays and other works that help us know his thinking about many subjects, including art. Vergil left only his poetry. Much of the interpretative project surrounding Vergil's works has been about what he reveals on the subject of art through his art.

In book six of the *Aeneid*, Aeneas descends to the Underworld to visit his dead father and learn the future of this Rome that Aeneas is charged by fate to establish. The book opens with a carved scene depicting the story of Daedalus. Daedalus had made wings of wax by which he could fly through the sky, but his son Icarus ignored his father's warning not to fly too close to the sun lest the wax wings melt. Icarus fell to the earth and died. Daedalus's sculptural relief of that story ends without his completing the images of his son's death. The craftsman had failed in his craft, and the poet/craftsman Vergil writes of that failure. In doing so, Vergil signals his own fear of failing to write the whole truth of his story (Putnam 1987).

While in Hades, Aeneas's father tells him the mission of the future Rome: "to spare the conquered and war down [*debellare*] the proud."[1] Yet in the very last lines of the poem in book 12, Aeneas has the choice, and we know from the lines that he knows he has the choice, to kill his humbled but formerly relentless enemy, or to spare him. Aeneas chooses to kill.

Considering together the artistic question that Vergil engraved in the Daedalus scene and the ethical question in the poem's final lines, we can posit that the poet established a framework for scrutinizing an ultimate moral dilemma. Vergil wants us to know that he may have failed on that ethical standard. The tradition that Vergil wanted to burn the epic, which was a prompt for Broch's *The Death of Virgil*, gains relevance from the evidence within the poem.

History may confirm Vergil's fears about the access of his poetry to ethics. The Battle of Actium secured Octavian's power. But did the perceived significance of the battle precede Vergil's description of it on Aeneas's shield in book 8 of the *Aeneid*, or did Vergil himself create the ideology of Actium and hence of the Augustan regime? Gurval (1995, 213) argues that the contemporary understanding of Actium as the beginning of a new age is Vergil's creation. If this is accurate, then Vergil's fears about the ethical implications of his work were justified. Also Johnson:

> It was the passionate concern and the imagination of Vergil that supplied an intellectual coherence to a period of time that would otherwise have lacked it, and of the few contemporaries of Vergil who cared about that coherence, Augustus took from it only what interested him.
>
> (Johnson 1976, 136)

The dying desperate poet of Broch's novel does not exaggerate the ancient poet's ethical worry about his poem's potential futures that he could not control, be they Augustan or modern. As Broch's Vergil said, quoted at the beginning of my first chapter, "only the agreeable things would be abstracted from it."[2]

Many of the epic's battle scenes, especially in the second half of the poem, also demonstrate Vergil's ambivalence about his possible role in establishing the Augustan ideology. Many scenes are intense, even horrifying because we have been led to know and care for the victims and also, sometimes especially, for their killers. We sense as well the poet's own abhorrence at the depravity of human slaughter, as Vergil says near the end of the epic: what god could explain slaughters in song?[3] Readers locate Vergil's integrity in the extreme of these depictions.

> The garden [of Epicurus] was impossible because [Vergil] could not teach himself not to hear the screams and riot outside. . . . Terrified though he was, he stood firm to report what he saw, and, as the poem

bears witness, the depth of his terror is the index of the greatness of his courage.

(Johnson 1976, 153)

Did we not know that the author was discussing the Roman Vergil, the description would aptly suit Broch's Vergil's terror and abhorrence of the mania that Augustus inspires in the crowds that adore him, his "awareness of the people's profound capacity for evil." Cox (1997, 331) describes Broch's Vergil similarly, "As if to recognize the failure of his life's work were not enough, a still more horrifying realization dawns upon Virgil, that the words which he has written will play their part in the barbaric wars that human beings wage against each other."

Like Broch, Vergil knew his power and his risks as a poet. In the Trojan horse episode of the *Aeneid*'s second book, a Greek soldier, Sinon, persuades his enemy Trojans to breach their city's walls and take the horse inside Troy. Sinon is an artful performer, pretending to be the victim of the Greeks and thus in harmony with the Trojans. His lies succeed; they precipitate the destruction of Troy. In this episode, Vergil tells us that the Trojans were defeated not by some great warrior, not by a ten-year war, not by a thousand ships, but by the treachery of words and the art of lies.[4] It is of course Vergil who wrote Sinon's lies, plus the commentary on them.

Broch's awareness of the power of art merges with ethical concerns, "Like hardly any other poet of the modern age, however, Broch endeavors to place the aesthetic back under the primacy of the ethical"; "The word duty (*Pflicht*) flows just as often from his mouth as from Augustus" (Heizmann 2003, 197 and 195). Duty, or piety, is also the main attribute of the ancient Vergil's hero Aeneas, *sum pius Aeneas,*[5] I am pious Aeneas, *pius* meaning something like religious duty to a calling greater than oneself. Duty is central in both works.

At one point in the novel, Broch calls artistic beauty a "game" and thus cruel:

> the game of earthly men amidst their earthliness, playing at eternity
> . . .
> and hence pitiless,
> pitiless toward human sorrow which meant no more to art
> than passing existence, no more than a word, a stone, a sound, . . .
> and thus beauty revealed itself to man as cruelty.

(*DoV* 122–123)

Broch was ethically conflicted about being a novelist and turned towards theoretical research and political action. He considered his novel writing a diversion from the responsibilities of his time, and himself a failure aware of failing to do any good in reality, like Daedalus in book 6. The intensity of feeling in the *Aeneid* relates to Vergil's awareness of the problem of making suffering into art. Just as Vergil's artistic integrity consisted in portraying the horrors humans create and also in questioning his own poetic project to do so, Broch's *The Death of Virgil* "calls his work into question through his protagonist Virgil" (Heizmann 2003, 196).

> *The Death of Virgil* pivots around Virgil's eventual realization that he has contributed to this infernal confusion by presenting through the *Aeneid* a lie which he asks his readers to accept as reality, namely the glorious beauty of empire. Broch has projected into the legend of Virgil's demand that the *Aeneid* should be burnt his own modernist awareness of the inadequacy and dishonesty of art.
>
> (Cox 1997, 328)

I would demur from this description only regarding the word "projected"; rather, the awareness Cox labels as modernist was actually Vergilian as well.

Just as Gurval and Johnson credit (or accuse) Vergil of advancing the creation of Augustan ideology, so Broch is criticized for doing what he abhorred, indulging in linguistic craft, "this prose is permeated with a pathetic contentment, a certain artistic triumph. . . . With this incantational tone . . . Broch sometimes runs the risk of celebrating only his own linguistic acrobatics" (Heizman 2003, 192). But on the other hand, Broch, like Vergil, knew his risks and sought to forestall them.

> wherever beauty existed for its own sake, there art is attacked at its very roots . . . his poetry could no longer be called art . . . it had been a mere indulgence of beauty . . . beauty in the place of truth . . . locked in the prison of art, thus was the poet condemned to fail from the start.
>
> (*DoV* 140–143)

Through his Vergil novel, as Vergil did through his *Aeneid*, Broch questioned his art and his role as artist.

As several of my colleagues in this book have noted, Theodor Adorno named the problem of art at mid-century: "To write poetry after Auschwitz is barbaric" (1983). Merely by existing, does art support structures of power and their abuses? A reader of Broch expressed the problem as follows, words that could have applied to Vergil as well as Broch: "Measured against the reality of suffering, art is both inadequate and incapable of giving voice to horror and agony, or it is complicit in it" (Paik 2003, 201). Inadequate, incapable, or complicit—those were Broch's and Vergil's perceived choices.

Yet I find neither artist to have lied or failed. The key to their success rests in their artistic styles, so different in appearance, but producing a similar effect. Through the style as much as the content of their works each responds to his history and says true things.

History as Style

The manifold and deep confusions in the eras of Vergil and Broch led to fundamental questions about the human capacity to make sense of the world. Broch's novel helps one to apply the discontinuities of Vergil's age to his poetry. For both artists, style encompasses the question of how to say philosophically reliable truth in poetic form. For both Broch and Vergil, the history is inscribed in the style.

> and in the *flawlessly* wrought and carved litter-seat . . . spangled with stars of goldleaf, rested a *flaw-infected* invalid in whom decay was already lurking. This all made for extreme *incongruity*.
>
> (*DoV* 29, emphases added)

This one compact example names a crucial attribute of Broch's style in the novel—incongruity. The simultaneous existence of opposite realities is literally embodied in Broch's ancient, dying poet, as, flaw-infected himself, he rests on a flawless piece of carving—human rot on perfect art. This creation and management of contradictory perceptions also marks Vergil's epic, famously described as the "two voices" of the *Aeneid* (Parry 1963), by which one event or image is depicted in different, even opposite ways. As Matthew Caleb Flamm indicates in his first chapter here, one effect of Plato's quarrel has been to inject an absolute dualism in Western thinking. Vergil's *Aeneid* already challenges that dualism.

Broch's novel has been said to anticipate later major strands of Vergil criticism, emphasizing the epic's multiple voices, its moral ambiguities, and the poet's artistic doubts (Thomas 2001, 261; Cox 1997, 335). Two sets of episodes illustrate the *Aeneid*'s presentation of situations from opposing points of view: the Dido story and that of the young warriors Nisus and Euryalus. The love story between Dido and Aeneas first occupies book four of the epic. The Trojans and Aeneas their leader are shipwrecked and seek the aid of Queen Dido of nearby Carthage, which she fully grants. Alas for her, a love affair ensues. Alas for Aeneas, his attachment to Dido and her rising city overshadows his fated duty to the future Rome, and he is called away by the gods from there and her. Aeneas handles his farewell oddly and coldly. Dido is maddened and commits suicide. Aeneas and we meet Dido again in book six, as Aeneas visits the Underworld and encounters Dido's shade. In a scene that has been shown to be verbally and emotionally a nearly exact opposite of Aeneas's farewell to her, Dido treats Aeneas as he had treated Dido (Skinner 1983). The result is that we the epic's audience see this one situation from the opposing points of view of its two participants. Is one view truer than the other?

A similar set of scenes involves the Trojan youths Nisus and Euryalus, in books 5 and 9, with opposite results, at first comic and then deadly. In book five the Trojans celebrate with sporting events the funeral of Aeneas's father Anchises. Aeneas oversees the games with benevolent equanimity. Nisus and Euryalus are contestants in the foot race, in which one of them stumbles badly and the other cheats to help him, but finally everyone has a good laugh. Thereafter, in book nine, the Trojans are at war in Italy. Nisus and Euryalus volunteer together for a dangerous night mission and meet initial success. Through over-eagerness for glory and spoils, including a helmet that reflects the moonlight, they are discovered by the enemy. One is mortally wounded, the other risks his life and is himself killed, dying over the body of his friend. What in book five was an amusing incident of youthful excess, in book nine, due to similar actions, costs the boys their lives. Two stories, Dido and Aeneas, Nisus and Euryalus, display the impossibility of a settled and simple interpretation of events, emotions, and values.

This type of confusion virtually defines the hero Aeneas. He is at times portrayed as a new Achilles (the main Greek hero from Homer's *Iliad*), or sometimes as Hector, Achilles's major Trojan enemy. At times Aeneas and his opponent in Italy, Turnus, reflect now Achilles and now Hector, changing the audience's perspective on them as hero or victim. They seem eventually to merge, for example in the simile near the end of the poem in which both are equally compared to bulls in combat (*Aen.* 12.715–722). Sometimes Aeneas seems an Augustus, and sometimes seems to be Augustus's civil war opponent Mark Antony.

Another complex aspect of the epic is its portrayal of time (e.g., Mack 1978). The epic relates the very ancient founding of a community, immediately after the Trojan war, that hundreds of years later would become Vergil's Rome. The epic portrays events which from its narrative perspective will occur in the future. Most of those events, however, comprise the actual history and experience of the audience. Time jumbles and meaning echoes. Now here is Broch's strange description of time for the dying poet.

> [E]very station on the path might encompass in itself the entire future and the entire past, arrested in the song of the unique present, bearing the moment of complete freedom, the moment of god-becoming, this time-free moment from which, nevertheless, the whole world would be embraced as a single, timeless memory.
>
> (*DoV* 45)

In history's moments when the world seems "upside down," time itself is unsettled, a victim of events that cannot be made sensible, but instead bounce off deep cultural memories. "[T]ime was balanced on a knife-edge," says Broch (*DoV* 51), as it was for Vergil. The spirit of the age for both was, in Broch's words, no longer and not yet (*DoV* 61, etc.), *noch nicht und doch schon.*[6]

The *Aeneid*'s contradicting stories and characters resonate internally in their oppositions, and we find his structures and connections brilliant and fascinating. But more than that, the strangeness of Broch's modern novel highlights the strangeness in the very old *Aeneid*, where meaning is not merely complex and oppositional but unstable, upside-down. For one reader Vergil "is stranger and less classical even in the *Aeneid* than he came to be, just as Shakespeare was stranger than he has come to be through four centuries of performance, reading, and teaching" (Thomas 2001, 15). William Gahan's chapter on Shakespeare's sonnets presents a similar interpretation of those poems as portraying and balancing opposite points of view.

Broch took the novel form beyond its traditional limits as Vergil did Homeric epic. The two artists responded similarly to an implied question: how to represent a world upside down other than by upending language and form. This novel barely tells a story; this poem so radically imitates its Homeric model[7] as to enshrine and obliterate it in simultaneous contradiction. The simultaneity of contrary views on reality and truth along with artistic strangeness mark both times and both works in ways we consider essentially modern. The radical work of the Peruvian poet Pimentel, discussed in Chapter 7 of this volume by John Burns, shares a kindred spirit confronting similar issues as did the Austrian novelist Hermann Broch, 58 years his senior, and the Roman poet Vergil, 2,000 years before them both.

Broch's anti-structural language creates a similarly destabilizing effect as Vergil's highly structured form (see, e.g., Duckworth 1962). Broch's language in *The Death of Virgil* can be dizzying; it seems to abandon syntax. One reader finds that Broch went further than James Joyce in Broch's "attempt to surpass the border of the modern novel" (Lützeler 2003, 9). The structural density of the *Aeneid*, by the end, similarly totters on the edge of manageability. Informed and sensitive readers of the *Aeneid* report reactions that seem more appropriate to the modern work than the ancient: the *Aeneid* in part "makes my head swim" (Fagles 2001, 177); it "shatters [its] genre" (Johnson 1981, 53). These expressions reflect especially the very end of the epic, which has been building for 10,000 lines in ever accumulating tension (Most 2001, 155).

The Death of Virgil recreates across several hundred pages the startling experience of the *Aeneid*'s final few lines. Richard Thomas expresses the intimacy between novel and poem; the novel "has the effect of eliding the millennia between the two writers" (2001, 262). The epic builds brick by brick accumulating into an explosion of meaning at the very end. *The Death of Virgil* expresses the explosion, and its bricks are spread out like high art debris. *The Death of Virgil* is the *Aeneid* inside out.[8]

The last words of Broch's novel capture the essential incongruity of the entire work: *"das Wort . . . jenseits der Sprache*," "the word beyond speech." About the *Aeneid*, in another example of uncanny resonance, the poet Rosanna Warren (2001, 114) says that "Vergil's art . . . in its most stringent form consists of *not* saying, an art of the unspoken, perhaps of the unspeakable (*infandum*)." Broch and Vergil exploded their artistic forms, while the makers of history were exploding history.

Broch's novel strengthens the reading not only of the ancient epic's historical immediacy but also of its artistic radicalism. We recall T.S. Eliot's declaration of the *Aeneid* as "the classic of all Europe" (1957, 73); the *Aeneid* and Vergil's other works permeate and define much of the European literary tradition. But there is another function as classic that the *Aeneid* may have performed, in its day, as Broch's Vergil performs it in the novel.

The novel is a meditation on death, "the death of a culture; the death of the artist; the death of art" (Lipking 1981, 131). Broch's Vergil foresees the end of the culture he himself founded; Broch "put the recanting of Western civilization into Virgil's own mouth" (Lipking 1981, xi and 136). The ancient Vergil, I think, knew that he was doing something similar (Johnson 1976, 91). Perhaps the depths of grief in the epic intuit the similar death, not just of the Roman Republic but of the world of values and assumptions understood from Homer on. Dodds (1959, 247) sees Vergil's first century BCE as the time when "the tide of rationalism . . . begins to retreat." Johnson (1976, 136) thinks that in the *Aeneid* Vergil "ponders the tragic failure of classical humanism." About Europe, Schorske (1981, 22) says that artists during Broch's age faced "the dissolution of the classical liberal view" of humankind. The exploded language of the novel and the epic's final narrative explosion evoke the political and intellectual histories of their authors. The artistic extremes of the two works recreate the extremity of their authors' lived experience.

A Place for Art

In reflecting on Plato's quarrel between poetry and philosophy, I have focused on the experience and expression of opposing, contradictory truths in ancient Rome and early twentieth-century Europe, in Vergil and Broch. One of Plato's arguments in his poetry and philosophy quarrel relates to the impossibility of contradictions being true: "And didn't we say that it is impossible for the same thing to believe opposites about the same thing at the same time" (Reeve, *Rep.* 10.602e). But this is exactly what Vergil does, writ large or small (Perkel 2001, 64), as does Broch.

Broch's modernist language resonates with characteristics difficult to name but widely attributed to Vergil, especially in the *Aeneid*, such as suspension, duality, indeterminacy, and the simultaneous portrayal of opposites or contradictions. Broch similarly grasps towards representing in words that kind of abstraction.

> [O]h, dusk, the hour of poetry. For poetry was contemplative waiting in the twilight, was at once participation and loneliness, was intermingling and the fear of intermingling, unwanton in intermingling, as unwanton as the dream of slumbering herds and yet the fear of wantonness; oh, poetry was anticipation but not quite departure, yet it was an enduring farewell.
>
> (*DoV* 65)

Broch's efforts evoke a similar aesthetic and intellectual response as the *Aeneid* does, despite the 2,000 years that separate them.

Stanley Rosen comments (1993, 77) that since ambiguity is inherent in human experience; poetry, which embraces ambiguity, must win the quarrel with philosophy, "one can no more banish ambiguity from philosophy than one can exclude it from human life." In that light, Rosen worries that philosophy might be impossible (ix), just as Vergil and Broch worry about poetry. Rosen also proposes a solution. It sounds strange; it is strange. Rosen says, "The possibility of philosophy stands or falls upon the possibility of a philosophical madness that is more sober than sobriety" (xiii): sober madness. This philosopher's language resonates in its strange sense of oppositional reality with the language and style of Vergil and Broch.

The Death of Virgil and the *Aeneid* offer a way to view the philosophical quarrel artistically, where the mutually contradictory binary nature of the quarrel ceases without resolving into a partial solution, and where the morality of art in immoral times is possible. Ultimately our two authors found a poetic solution to this philosophical problem.

Upside-down-ness is written into the *Aeneid*. This claim seems self-evidently different from one's expectation of the highly organized and methodical epic. The Latin language itself is orderly, with elegant grammatical paradigms that for people who love language are satisfying. In addition, the epic's structures are massive but decipherable and thus reassuring. The structures themselves created the order that Roman history then lacked. Then the *Aeneid*'s ending seems to blow it all up. Similarly the poet who emerges in *The Death of Virgil* is shorn of millennia-old rational structures of language and thought, and, with them, assurance that the world's empires and their arts can reflect a rational universe.

Rosanna Warren's wonderful poem on Turnus tells us the *Aeneid*'s ending "tears a hole in the poem, a hole in the mind" (1995–96, 174). In reading Broch's novel, we live for many pages inside that experiential hole, that artistic space. That is where, I believe, for Vergil and Broch, a "space" exists for opposites to be simultaneously true.

The novelist Margaret Anne Doody expresses the upside-down-ness of the end of the Roman Republic as it relates to the experience of reading the epic, "Aeneas and his companions are living in the crack, on the cusp between times and worlds. . . . This is a good nowhere situation in which to go crazy" (2001, 192). Of *The Death of Virgil*, one reader says that Broch's "Virgil declares this location between two shores of time to be the genuine site of the poet" (Heizmann 2003, 194).

These readers across disciplines articulate virtually identical aesthetic experiences in works that cross millennia.[9] It is for this reason, among others, that readers often characterize Vergil's works, ancient as they are, as nonetheless modern. For the scholar Otis (1964, 3), "What did [Vergil] do so that . . . an obvious imitation of Homer could become the true epic of a metropolis [ancient Rome] that has vastly more in common with contemporary New York than the [Homeric cities of] Mycenae or Tiryns?" Another the poet Karl Kirchway finds *Aeneid* not only modern, but postmodern in its sensibility (2010, 100).

The following statements display an undeniably postmodern tone. The first, by the twentieth-century philosopher Jacques Derrida (1997), does not refer to the *Aeneid* or to *The Death of Virgil*, but could be applied to either of them. He is discussing a concept or place that "provokes and resists any binary . . . determination" (19), of which he says, "didn't it name a gaping opening, an abyss or a chasm? . . . that cleavage between the sensible and the intelligible" (20). Here is another example, also not about Vergil and Broch but apt to their method, "The voices remain multiple, at best echoing one another, generating a play of echoes through which the [work] . . . makes something manifest, yet without producing simple univocity. In their multiplicity the voices are interactive, peculiarly performative" (Sallis 1999, 1). In both cases, the authors are referring, not to modern or postmodern literature or philosophy, but to a very ancient work, older than Vergil's—to Plato's dialogue *Timaeus*.

> [F]or whereas then we distinguished two Forms, we must now declare another third Kind. For our former exposition those two were sufficient, one of them . . . a Model Form . . . , intelligible and everywhere uniformly existent, and the second as the model's Copy, subject to becoming and visible.
>
> (Bury, *Tim.* 48e–49a)[10]

Plato is restating his idea of forms, of a binary ideational state of things or concepts that we can experience, however, only as copies of the ideal. But in the *Timaeus* Plato modifies the world he invented of absolute and unmixable opposites, ideal and real, and creates a "third kind" in addition to the previous two.

> [A]nd a third kind is ever-lasting Place . . . itself being a kind of bastard reasoning by the aid of non-sensation, barely an object of belief; for when we regard this we dimly dream and affirm that it is somehow necessary that all that exists should exist *in* some spot and occupying some *place* . . . neither on earth nor anywhere in the Heaven.
>
> (Bury, *Tim.* 52 a-b)

It turns out that Plato himself sounds postmodern.

These ancient and modern philosophers are articulating a key aspect of the styles of our two artists—one ancient, one modern: the constant interplay of opposite and contradictory images and ideas until the accumulation seems to explode old form and occupy a new place. Broch's style is an extreme instance of the explosion of traditional structures and ideas found in much modern and postmodern art and thought. The final explosion in the *Aeneid* does the same thing. Broch's modernity, it turns out, accurately reflects Vergil's radicalism.

Here then, in Plato's idea of some place—the Greek word is *chôra*—for the existence of opposites before they are reified is a Platonic answer to the Platonic problem this volume addresses, the quarrel between poetry and philosophy. We have reached this philosophic answer through poetic exposition. The success of the response occurs through art; the comprehension and naming of the response is philosophic.[11]

Both our artists create an experience that is true to their similar moments in history. Both works of art strengthen their audiences, even as their histories self-destruct. Art itself and perhaps alone encompasses both the destruction and the means for truthful ethical survival and construction, preserving, despite heavy historical odds, the capacity to tell the whole truth. In this light, poetry answers fully Plato's challenge to it, as Flamm indicates in the first chapter, "to be not only pleasant but also beneficial."

Notes

1. Fairclough (1994), *Aen.* 6.853, *parcere subiectis et debellare superbos.* All references to the *Aeneid* are in this edition. The Latin word for war is *bellum*; the verb *debellare* means literally to war down, in effect to wear down through war.

2. This issue of whether Vergil's poetry reflected Actian ideology or created it echoes the distinction made several times in this book between poetic making and philosophic discovering. Did Vergil create, make that ideology, or did he perceive and name, that is discover, a current reality?

3. *Aen.* 12.500–3, *Quis mihi nunc tot acerba deus, quis carmine caedes . . . expediat*: What god might now explain for me so many horrible things, slaughters in song. Fairclough (1996).

4. *Aen.* 2.195–98, *Talibus insidiis periurique arte Sinonis / credita res, captique dolis lacrimisque coactis / quos neque Tydides nec Larissaeus Achilles; non anni domuere decem, non mille carinae.*

5. This is how Aeneas introduces himself to Dido, Queen of Carthage, *Aen.* 1.373. The adjective is used of Aeneas consistently throughout the epic. See also William Gahan in this volume on Sidney's reading of Vergil's Aeneas and virtue.

6. I note the resonance between this phrase and that of William James as cited by Matthew Caleb Flamm: the "ever not quite."

7. Flamm's first chapter cites Gould on quasi-philosophical issues in ancient Greek poetry before Plato articulated them. See for example, Michael Naas (1995) on turning to philosophy from rhetoric, where his discussion seems akin to ours on philosophy and poetry. The notion of a "turn" this time back to poetry recurs in Flamm's second chapter here, regarding Heidegger. A long historical trail from Homer to current issues in art and philosophy is adumbrated in our volume.

8. For a theoretical approach to two-way readings across time, see Pogorzelski (2016). In general on reader response and reception theories as used in classical studies, see, e.g., Martindale and Farrell (2006) and Hardwick and Stray (2008).

9. In his first chapter, Flamm cites a similar point in Santayana: "When poetry achieves its aim . . . it is an opening into reality exactly at the margins of interpretation."

10. I am reminded here of Gahan's discussion of More as "playfully mixing them on purpose" regarding the attributes of poetry and philosophy.

11. Elsewhere I hope to explore the connection between Plato's *chôra* and Vergil's Arcadia in the *Eclogues*.

References

Adorno, Theodor. 1983. *Prisms*. Translated by S. and S. Webber. Cambridge, MA: MIT.

Broch, Hermann. 1995. *The Death of Virgil: A Novel*. Translated by Jean Starr Untermeyer. Random House. New York.

Bury, Robert Gregg trans. 1989. *Plato in Twelve Volumes. IX. Timaeus, Critias, Cleitophon, Menexenus, Epistles*. Harvard.

Cox, Fiona. 1997. "Envoi: The Death of Virgil." In *The Cambridge Companion to Virgil*, edited by Charles Martindale. Cambridge.

Derrida, Jacques. 1997. *Chora L Works*. Edited by Jeffrey Kipnis and Thomas Lesser. Monacelli Press.

Dodds, Eric Robertson 1959. *The Greeks and the Irrational*. California.

Doody, Margaret Anne. 2001. "Lacrimae rerum: The Influence of Vergil Virtual Roundtable, with participation by Karl Kirchwey, J. D. McClatchy, Kenneth

Haynes, Paul Alpers, Paul A. Cantor, Glenn Most, Margaret Anne Doody)." In *Poets and Critics Read Vergil*, edited by Sarah Spence. Yale, 191–193.

Duckworth, George E. 1962. *Structural Patterns and Proportions in Vergil's Aeneid*. Michigan.

Eliot, T.S. 1957. "What is a Classics?" In *On Poetry and Poets*. New York, 52–74.

Fagles, Robert. 2001. "Vergil Reading Homer (in conversation with Sarah Spence)." In *Poets and Critics Read Vergil*, edited by Sarah Spence. Yale, 172–183.

Fairclough, Rushton H. 1994 and 1996. *Vergil I* and *Vergil II*. Harvard.

Gurval, Robert Alan. 1995. *Actium and Augustus. The Politics and Emotions of Civil War*. Michigan.

Hardwick, Lorna and Christopher Stray. 2008. *A Companion to Classical Receptions*. Blackwell.

Heizmann, Jürgen. 2003. "A Farewell to Art: Poetic Reflection in Broch's *Der Tod des Vergil*." In *Hermann Broch, Visionary in Exile. The 2001 Yale Symposium*, edited by Paul Michael Lützeler, 187–200. Camden House.

Johnson, W. Ralph 1976. *Darkness Visible. A Study of Vergil's Aeneid*. California.

Johnson, W. Ralph 1981. "The Broken World. Virgil and His Augustus." *Arethusa* 14.1, 49–56.

Kirchwey, Karl. 2010. Cited in Joseph Farrell and Michael Putnam, eds., *A Companion to Vergil's Aeneid and its Tradition*. Wiley-Blackwell, 100.

Lipking, Lawrence. 1981. *The Life of the Poet: Beginning and Ending of Poetic Careers*. Chicago.

Lützeler, Paul Michael. 2003. "Introduction: Broch, Our Contemporary." In *Hermann Broch, Visionary in Exile. The 2001 Yale Symposium*, edited by Paul Michael Lützeler, 1–10. Camden House.

Mack, Sara. 1978. *Patterns of Time in Vergil*. Archon Books, Hamden, CT.

Martindale, Charles and Richard F. Thomas. 2006. *Classics and the uses of Reception*. Blackwell.

Most, Glenn W. 2001. "Memory and Forgetting in the *Aeneid*." *Vergilius* 47, *Special Issue: The Vergilian Century*, 148–170.

Naas, Michael. 1995. *Turning: From Persuasion to Philosophy. A Reading of Homer's Iliad*. Humanities Press.

Otis, Brooks. 1964. *Virgil: A Study in Civilized Poetry*. Oxford.

Paik, Peter Yoosuk. 2003. "Poetry as Perjury." In *Hermann Broch, Visionary in Exile. The 2001 Yale Symposium*, edited by Paul Michael Lützeler. Camden House, 201–216.

Parry, Adam. 1963. "The Two Voices of Virgil's *Aeneid*." *Arion* 2.4 (Winter 1963), 66–80.

Perkell, Christine. 2001. "Vergil Reading His Twentieth-Century Readers: A Study of *Eclogue 9*." *Vergilius* 47, *Special Issue: The Vergilian Century*, 64–88.

Pogorzelski, Randall J. 2016. *Virgil and Joyce. Nationalism and Imperialism in the Aeneid and Ulysses*. Wisconsin.

Putnam, Michael C.J. 1987. "Daedalus, Virgil and the End of Art." *AJPh* 108, 173–198.

Reeve, C.D.C. 2004. *Plato. Republic*. Hackett.

Rosen, Stanley. 1993. *The Quarrel Between Philosophy and Poetry: Studies in Ancient Thought.* Routledge.

Sallis, John. 1999. *Chorology. On Beginning in Plato's Timaeus.* Indiana.

Schorske, Carl E. 1981. *Fin-de-Siècle Vienna. Politics and Culture.* Vintage Books, Random House.

Skinner, Marilyn B. 1983. "The Last Encounter of Dido and Aeneas: *Aen.* 6.450–476." *Vergilius* 29, 12–18.

Thomas, Richard F. 2001. *Virgil and the Augustan Reception.* Cambridge.

Warren, Rosanna. 1995–96. "Turnus (*Aeneid* XII)." *Arion* 3.2/3, 174.

Warren, Rosanna. 2001. "The End of the *Aeneid.*" In *Poets and Critics Read Vergil,* edited by Sarah Spence, 105–117. New Haven.

7 Jorge Pimentel

Obfuscation for Clarity's Sake

John Burns

What does language hide and what does it reveal? What gets lost between idea and execution in the process of creating? As discussed elsewhere in this book, variations on these questions are common in both the ancient quarrel between poetry and philosophy as well as contemporary considerations of the debate in the works of Heidegger, among others. In this chapter, I extend our examination of the ancient quarrel to include a consideration of twentieth-century experimental poetry. Specifically, I will be looking at the work of Jorge Pimentel, a member of Hora Zero, a group of poets in Peru who began publishing their work in the early 1970s. Hora Zero sought to invigorate the language of Peruvian poetry, and Pimentel's work within the group could be read as a microcosm for twentieth-century poetry in general: by turns, it was open and accessible and then hermetic and markedly difficult. In the movement between clarity and difficulty, Pimentel's work not only embodies many contemporary debates around lyric poetry but is in itself a contemporary variation on the ancient quarrel between poetry and philosophy.

At first glance, the ancient and contemporary traditions seem incommensurable. Before looking for some commonalities between bodies of thought produced in Athens around 350 BCE and literary movements born in Peru circa 1970 CE, it is worth emphasizing the obvious: there are huge differences between the avant-garde and Platonic philosophy. However, taken as theories of language, what the traditions of Platonic philosophy and neo-avant-garde poetry have in common is that they are both founded on a form of profound mistrust about the ability of language to engage with truth. For Plato, poetic language has great potential for the perception of the original ideas. The underlying assumption is that language represents reality and falters as it does so. For the historical avant-garde, and for subsequent neo-avant-garde movements, there were elements of the referential quality of language that rendered it suspect. The underlying assumption is that language does not represent reality but instead constitutes it to some degree, and falters as it does so. How does poetic language come up short for both Plato and Pimentel?

The work of Thomas Gould provides further insight into the nature of that mistrust. Earlier in the book Matthew Flamm pointed out that "the grandiosity of Gould's thesis may have deficiencies." Nevertheless, despite some of the potential oversimplifications of Gould's claims, his framework can be useful in thinking through certain aspects of the quarrel that remain resonant with the work of Pimentel. Gould situates the quarrel as fundamentally related to the notion of *pathos* and the mistrust that arises before the powerful emotions that *poesis* elicits. Gould situates Plato's mistrust in terms of the perversity of pathos. Furthermore, Gould call the quarel "a permanent state of affairs" (1990, xxvi) and sides largely with poetry, referring to the *Odyssey* and the *Iliad* as the originator of both poetry and philosophy. He situates Plato's claims against imitative poetry in terms of addiction and base desire:

> Hence, imitative poetry, like painting, is indeed superficial, for it appeals to the part of us that is drawn to images only. . . . Plato is inviting us to see that the good man, one who insists on rational control in the misfortunes that occur in his own life, may file into the Theater of Dionysus, take his seat among rows of people all sitting silently, all turned in the same direction, then switch his intelligence off and give free rein to a part that is normally in command only in his dreaming. No wonder we find ourselves enjoying scenarios in tragedy that we could never contemplate with pleasure in our own lives! Plato tells us, moreover, that the experience is addictive, that we risk making this inversion permanent. We would then have a state of affairs exactly analogous to a city governed wholly by its worst element.

> (1990, 32)

For Plato, poetic language is a degradation of the truth and the word inevitably strays far from the original idea. Something has taken over which should not have done so: emotion, pleasure, compulsion.

If Gould emphasizes Plato's mistrust in terms of the emotional instability of the consumer, be it listener, reader or spectator, of poetry, Stanley Rosen deepens the argument in terms of the nefarious abilities of language itself. He reminds us that "[i]f we take the term (poiēsis) in its extended sense of 'production,' the question of writing is clearly a specific instance of a more general issue" (1993, 1). Within that "more general issue," he places the role of licentiousness as second to poetry's ability to manipulate the truth. Poetry puts forth "falsehoods masquerading as the truth. Second, poetry is morally or politically defective because it encourages the license of desire, and, in particular, of Eros" (1993, 1). Furthermore, the deformation and oversimplification of the idea is the quintessential defect of mimetic art. The deficiencies of mimetic art for Plato lie in the fact that it cannot produce a concretion of the original ideas because, upon verbalizing them, they are immediately rendered as mere imitation. Language becomes a circular trap.

Looking at the twentieth-century avant-garde, we see that the impulse to smash that trap took on various forms in the 1910s and 1920s with the proliferation of "-isms" that sought to challenge language and poetic practice. The Dadaists, the Futurists in Italy, Russia (as well as the lesser-known Futurists of Poland), Imagists, Surrealists, and so on all sought a poetic language that did justice to the radical changes ushered in by the twentieth century. In the most general of terms, the avant-garde mistrust of representational language had to with the fact that the world had been turned upside down by technological advancement, death, and warfare on an unimaginable scale. Language cannot overcome its internal contradictions vis-à-vis reality. For the pre-modern and the postmodern, the language is differently but equally insufficient. For Plato, language represents (or fails to represent) reality. For experimental writers such as Pimentel, the representation of reality in language and the creation of reality in language are inextricable.

Gould suggests Plato mistrusted the pathos that disproportionately engaged the ancient Greek theatre spectator. The avant-garde critique of representational language accused it of disproportionately engaging an outdated, Romantic notion of a coherent, unified "I." As Marjorie Perloff says of experimental writing of the late twentieth century, one of the central principles of experimental poetics "has been the dismissal of 'voice' as the foundational principle of lyric poetry" (2004, 29). Both pathos and the "lyric I" can be construed as misleading oversimplifications. With a minimal shift in theoretical terminology, setting aside the chicken and egg argument of the representation versus the constitution of reality, the critical sentiments surrounding experimental poetry at the very least resonates with Plato's conception of creation through language. Contemporary experimental writing and the Platonic dialogs are warding off similar boogie men.

While Pimentel has a strong experimental vein in much of his work, he does go back and forth between a hermetic style, such as that of *Tromba de Agosto* (*August Cyclone*) first published in 1992 and a much more open, accessible style, as in *Ave Soul*, first published in 1973. Few poets embody this stylistic pendulum between the increasingly outmoded lyric "I" and the more fragmented, anti-lyrical thrust of the avant-garde quite as well as Pimentel, but one who certainly does so is the poetic and central intellectual forebear of Hora Zero: the great Peruvian poet of the first half of the twentieth century, César Vallejo. A towering figure in Spanish American letters, Vallejo moved between a highly hermetic, inaccessible style and a style that borders on conversational transparency. As Carlos Villacorta González writes:

> Hora Zero is fairly controversial in their manifestos and contradictory in their poetic proposals from the outset. Their self-naming as "the last Latin American poetic avant-garde" sounds quite like pride and egocentrism. Nevertheless, their search for aesthetic renovation meant a new outlook on Peruvian poetry, which was always tied to an urban, lettered and elitist group. Their need to introduce a new discourse into Peruvian poetry implied knocking down the belief in poetry as an action distanced from the revolutionary or social act. In this senses, Hora Zero draws near to later Vallejo, with distance to social participation and mobilization that the group in the seventies demanded.
>
> (2017, 45)[1]

Vallejo's most famous work is *Trilce*, published in 1922. It is full of neologisms and reflections on the nature of language, and deeply embodies the hermetic stylistic tendency. By way of one brief example, he writes in "Poem VI" of *Trilce*:

> My washerwoman has not washed
> The suit I wore tomorrow:
> She was washing it in her Otilian veins.
> (1922, 13)[2]

In addition to the peculiar mixing of past verb tenses with the adverb "tomorrow," he includes a seemingly opaque neologism, "Otilian," an adjective presumably based on the name of the washerwoman (Otilia). The poem unfolds along its own internal connections and linguistic playfulness to create an unstable text that reads like a series of thoughts springing into the poet's mind. This can be compared to the more transparent, declarative lyrical style in books like the posthumously published *España, aparta de mí este cáliz* (*Spain, take this cup from me*) (1939), which includes poems such as "Piedra negra sobre piedra blanca" ("White stone on black stone") in which he predicted his own death on a rainy Thursday in Paris.

In *Trilce*, with its magnificent mumblings, the poet seemed to be grasping towards an internal truth in moments of marked personal turmoil, including the deaths of his mother as well as a close friend, a romantic failure, and even a stint in jail. The Civil War in Spain, and, moreover, the impending threat of war in Europe, that Vallejo confronts in *España, aparta de mí este cáliz* elicited a more transparent style of poetry to deal with the matter at hand. Perhaps there was too much at stake in a collective sense to privilege the individualistic ruminations of a hermetic text like *Trilce*.

Pimentel's work clearly and directly dialogs with that of Vallejo. The group to which he belonged, Hora Zero, looked to Vallejo as a poetic and intellectual model to be followed, and in the particular case of Pimentel, it is nearly impossible to read his work without hearing direct echoes of his Peruvian forebear. Pimentel is, of course, hardly alone. There is a marked and consistent tendency in the Latin American neo-avant-garde to enter into dialogue with the earlier twentieth-century avant-garde.

In fact, to someone looking in from the outside at the Spanish-language traditions of experimental poetry, it might seem like droves of poets suddenly decided to give up on making sense in the late twentieth century and well into the twenty-first. Pronounced fragmentation, the dismantling of the lyric "I," and wild juxtapositions are at the fore. Among countless other poets who rose to prominence in the seventies, we could take as examples Cuban poet José Kozer and Chilean poet Raúl Zurita. In general terms, most readers of poetry likely would find both of these poets to be highly experimental. Kozer claims to have written over 10,000 poems, often employing a disjointed, neo-baroque style. Raúl Zurita, in the context of a military dictatorship, wrote poems which employed mixed media elements such as photographs, handwritten notes, and even a set of EEGs. This stylistic tendency is far from marginal: Kozer and Zurita, for example, were each awarded the prestigious Pablo Neruda Ibero-American Poetry Prize in 2013 and 2016, respectively.

As a group, Hora Zero's objective was to revitalize the poetry of Peru by introducing elements to it that they felt had been systematically excluded. As Carlos Villacorta González puts it, "Hora Zero sought to incorporate in their proposal a new type of poetry: one that was based on the experiences of migrants and those from the provinces" (2017, 40).[3] As with the literary movements I have mentioned previously, this group had a very particular set of circumstances that led them to question dominant modes of language in poetic practice. Like many Peruvians at the time who were immigrating for economic reasons, several members of the group came to Lima from other parts of the country in the latter decades of the twentieth century. For the members of Hora Zero, the cultural references and linguistic sensibilities of a certain class of poets in Lima had come to stand in almost entirely for Peruvian poetry as a whole, much to the detriment of other forms of expression. As another founder of the group, Tulio Mora, writes in the introductory essay to the 2009 anthology *Los broches mayores del sonido* (*The greater brooches of sound*), they sought to bring their peripheral cultural and linguistic sensibilities to bear in the urban center of Peru. Mora writes, "The urban transformation came together in those years"[4] (2009, 18) and the language on the margin of the nation is able to penetrate the center as migration to the city grows.

The tension in Pimentel's poetry between language as means to revelation and language as an inevitable obfuscation is further embedded in the tension between center and periphery in Peru. Poetic expression is caught up in a complex web of migration that integrates aesthetic concerns with considerations of political economics. He is at turns dense and cryptic and then, just as suddenly, playful and lyrical. He is utterly transparent and then appears to be mumbling to himself. Pimentel's attitudes about language and representation are perhaps best exemplified between the relatively direct and concise style of *Ave Soul* and the hermeticism of texts like the ones that make up *Tromba de agosto*.

Ave Soul creates the impression of being a very personal volume of poetry, written during a period of two years in which he was living in Spain. Roberto Bolaño, who would posthumously become a looming figure in Spanish American letters at a global level, discovered the work of Hora Zero in the early seventies and was so impressed that, when writing a manifesto for his own group of poets, the infrarrealistas,[5] he simply declared: "HORA ZERO came before us"[6] (2014, 383). With particular regard to *Ave Soul*, Bolaño found it to be one of the most remarkable volumes of poetry he had ever read, a continuation and permutation of the Whitmanic tradition of openness that can be found in Spanish American letters. He wrote:

> the path of *Ave Soul*, with those poems of a Whitmanic stock, but which are already something else altogether, with their extraordinary monologues . . . poems that go between soap operas and sociological documentaries, medieval ballads and a revision of socialist-realist novels, from manifesto . . . to manifestation, making the hybridity and the humor entirely his own.
>
> (Pimentel 2014, 12)[7]

In short, Bolaño was interested in Pimentel's work for the freshness of its direct observations shaped in relatively direct language, like Whitman celebrating himself in the grass, or asking in the Deathbed Edition of *Leaves of Grass* if the digestive problems of the elderly were worthy subjects of a poem. To paraphrase Whitman, both poets contain multitudes. *Ave Soul* is a book of a declarative nature that tries to measure and reflect the world in referential and transparent language.

One example of referentiality and transparency is the poem "14 entregas breves de amor y desarraigo para un musiquero con guitarra / balada" (14 brief installments of love and uprooting for a music lover with guitar / ballad). The poem presents a lyric "I" with a deep knowledge of the city, with all its cracks and fragmentations fused in a series of enumerated observations. Like Wallace Stevens in his "13 Ways of Looking at a Blackbird," the poem explores ways of seeing and the relationship between subject and object. The lyric "I"'s experience is expressed by means of the anaphor "To leave a city"[8] at the beginning of each of the 14 "installments." Pimentel writes: "To leave a city / its cemetery / with its tombs,"[9] or "To leave a city / Sunday / in the parks / where you shattered your foreigner's solitude" (Pimentel 2014, 117).[10] In the poem, the city is constructed on the basis of public spaces that suggest the experience of loss. Manufactured goods related to travel recur throughout the poem (umbrellas, suitcases, buses). Additionally, the experience of being out in the open is a constant throughout the lyric sequence (the rain, the sky, and the "luz y viento" ("light and wind")) of the final verses of the poem (Pimentel 2014, 125). The poem has a notable symmetry in the form of its stanzas, triangular cascades that assume a more or less similar form in each stanza. The repetition of forms, manufactured objects, and weather is represented with a paraphrasable narrative clarity.

This clarity is also present in the poem "La balada del hombre del siglo XXI" ("Ballad of the 21st century man"), one of several poems in *Ave Soul* that is labeled as a ballad, in other words, overtly narrative poems from not only a poetic tradition but also a popular musical tradition. This particular ballad, like many other poems in the book, bears witness to late capitalism in Lima. A lyric "I" that is at once immense and fragile narrates the story, anchored in themes of labor and exploitation. It begins: "I am the man, sought by justice like a needle in a haystack."[11] Pimentel goes on:

> And a wind floods me from head to toe, bringing me the smell of
> fresh-baked bread
> And I strum my guitar by the roadside.
> Those who feared facing the truth do not see the light.
> Those who put their knowledge in the hands of criminals do not see
> the light.
> To touch a body and light up the city, to not touch it and darken it.
> To not create individual sentiments but rather create collective sentiments.
> (Pimentel 2014, 65)[12]

The poem continues with a stanza that explains why the twenty-first century man walks:

> I walk to give food to the hungry, I walk.
> I walk to give drink to the thirsty, I walk.
> I walk to give cover to whoever does not have it, I walk.
> (Pimentel 2014, 65)[13]

As Carlos Villacorta González writes in his book *Poéticas de la ciudad: Lima en la poesía de los setenta* (*Poetics of the city: Lima in the poetry of the 60s*), walking in this poem not only renders the city legible, like Benjamin's figure of the flaneur, the person who makes sense of the city by wandering its streets. It also lifts the speaker out of his isolation: "caminar es la finalidad que une al yo con el otro, pues sólo en él es posible el encuentro" ("walking is the finality that unites self with other, since only then is meeting possible") (2017, 153).

To return this consideration of Pimentel, in some measure, to the matter of the ancient quarrel between poetry and philosophy, Stanley Rosen's reading of Plato might be helpful. Pimentel is offering up a direct, paraphrasable reflection of life in Lima in the seventies. It is an attempt to use language that is clear and concise to reflect and measure life in the city. In *The Quarrel Between Poetry and Philosophy*, Stanley Rosen analyzes the *Philebus* in which Socrates, during a conversation on the role of pleasure in life, leads Protrarchus to consider the role of mathematics in the arts. Along the way, he develops a definition of the *episteme* in the context of philosophy. Rosen writes:

> It is therefore evident that arithmetic, or counting, measuring and weighing, rules in the arts. This decision in turn follows from the assumption that episteme in its official or philosophical sense, means "precise knowledge" rather than "practical know how."
>
> (1993, 22)

What is the role of "precise knowledge" in poetry, both for Plato and Pimentel? As we noted before, for Plato, the defect of mimetic art consists, in large part, of its inability to produce a concretion of the original ideas. Upon verbalization, they are rendered mere imitations. If we attempted to translate this idea into more contemporary terms, we could say that the enumeration in the case of "14 entregas breves" or the conversational tone in "Balada del hombre del siglo XXI" is a simplification of the reality behind the words. It is a simplification that renders legible a perceiving subject (the lyric "I") who can perceive the city as a recent migrant and who can attempt to undertake the linguistic renovation that the founding members of Hora Zero proposed.

In the case of *Tromba de agosto*, Pimentel is no longer content with representative possibilities of referential and transparent language. If in *Ave Soul* the poet is imitating the world, inevitably reducing its complexities in the process to render it legible, in *Tromba de agosto*, Pimentel eschews faithfully imitated reality for the sake of highly complex and hermetic language that reflects the *process* of perception rather than perception itself.

As an example of the tendency in Pimentel's work, in "Aporte del pobre" ("Contribution of the poor person") Pimentel links up a series of apparently disjointed phrases:

> less weak than tickets,
> absorbent, Christian, arrogant,
> faithful, also fortuitous, charismatic,
> ennobled, cylindrical, thick, cubed
> . . .
>
> enclosed, on deaf ears, don't even count Friday
> on Monday firings, death Saturday, still
> benefactors, auditors, peaceful, spokesperson,
> suffixes, correct people, scavenger wolves.
>
> (2012, 165)[14]

What emerges is not a contribution from the poor person, as the title ironizes, but rather an assault on him. The chaotic string of images is a vision of the city dweller as poor, alienated and indebted. Instead of constructing a lyric "I" capable of narrating a clear experience, or of establishing a symmetrical lyrical sequence with public spaces, anaphoras and manufactured goods, the poem constructs an experience that would appear to lead to the dissolution of the poor person himself. The suffering of late capitalism obfuscates the coherence of the perceiving subject and reveals commodity fetishism, exploitation, and linguistic alienation. Through this obfuscation, the logic that emerges is the exclusive logic of the consumer society. The poem does not describe this exclusive logic—it enacts it through the difficulty of the poem, through its elisions and a relentless parade of apparently illogical associations.

Here, I suspect, Pimentel has come to the conclusion that "precise knowledge" in clear, transparent language could not do justice to the theme of the poem. The transparent poem cannot do the same justice to the pressures of contemporary life for the disenfranchised without making those pressures sound reasonable, logical, and inevitable. It would be a vain attempt to undo the master's house with the master's tools. Plato warned that poetry is morally defective for privileging desire above truth. If we consider the notion of the lyric "I" of the Romantic tradition as a form of desire, a desire for coherence that artistically validates the status quo, in *Tromba de agosto*, language itself enacts the condition of the urban subject which would have gotten buried in a simpler, more straightforward description. The steadier "lyric I" of the earlier work, *Ave Soul*, grants legibility and visibility to the provincial arriviste in Lima, as the poet writes, in order to "not create individual sentiments but rather create collective sentiments" (2012, 65). The immediate need for legibility and comprehension, like the political turmoil in Europe for Vallejo in *España aparta de mí este cáliz,* would not as easily allow for the fragmentary, challenging style of Pimentel's later work. The two books, read in dialogue, show that Pimentel's inner quarrel, centuries later and half a world away, bears more than a passing resemblance to the ancient quarrel between poetry and philosophy.

Notes

1. Hora Zero es un grupo bastante polémico en sus manifiestos y contradictorios en sus propuestas poéticas desde su aparición. Su auto-nombramiento como la "última vanguardia latinoamericana de poesía" suena mucho a soberbia y egocentrismo. Sin embargo, su búsqueda de renovación estética significó una nueva mirada a la poesía peruana que siempre estuvo ligada a un grupo elitista, letrado y urbano. Su necesidad de introducir un discurso nuevo en la poesía peruana implicó derrumbar la creencia de la poesía como una acción alejada del acto revolucionario o social. En este sentido, Hora Zero se acerca mucho al último Vallejo, con la distancia de participación y movilización social que el grupo del setenta reclamaba.
2. El traje que vestí mañana / no lo ha lavado mi lavandera: / lo lavaba en sus venas otilinas.
3. Hora Zero buscó incorporar en su propuesta un nuevo tipo de poesía: aquella que se basaba en las experiencias de los migrantes y provincianos.
4. La tranformación urbana se consolida en aquellos años.
5. "Déjenlo todo nuevamente" [Leave it all, once more] (1976).
6. Nos antecede HORA ZERO.
7. [E]l camino de *Ave Soul,* con esos poemas de estirpe whitmaniana, pero que ya eran otra cosa, con sus monólogos extraordinarios . . . poemas que transitan de la telenovela al documental sociológico, del romance medieval a la revisión de la novela realsocialista, del manifiesto . . . a la manifestación, haciendo suyo el hibridaje y el humor.
8. Dejar una ciudad.
9. Dejar una ciudad / su cementerio / con sus tumbas.
10. Dejar una ciudad / el domingo / en los parques / donde rompiste tu soledad de extranjero.
11. Soy el hombre, al que la justicia busca como una aguja en un pajar.
12. Y un viento me inunda de pies a cabeza, trayéndome un aroma de pan recién horneado / Y rasgo mi guitarra a la vera del camino. / No ven la luz cuantos temieron hacerle frente a la verdad. / No ven la luz cuantos pusieron su saber en manos criminales. / Tocar un cuerpo e iluminar la ciudad, no tocarlo y oscurecerlo. / No crear sentimientos individuales sino crear sentimientos colectivos.
13. Camino para dar de comer al hambriento, camino. / Camino para dar de beber al sediento, camino. / Camino para dar abrigo al que no tiene, camino.
14. menos débiles que boletos, / absorbentes, cristianos, arrogantes, / fidedignos, también fortuitos, carismáticos, / ennoblecidos, cilíndricos, espesos, cúbicos . . . / encierro, a oídos sordos, viernes ni lo cuentes, / a lunes despidos, a sábado muerte, todavía / benefactores, auditores, serenos, interlocutores, / sufijos, señores probos, lobos carroñeros.

92   *John Burns*

References

Bolaño, Roberto. 2014. "Déjenlo todo, nuevamente." In *Perros habitados por lasvoces del desierto*, edited by Rubén Medina, 381–387. Mexico City: Aldus.
Gould, Thomas. 1990. *The Ancient Quarrel Between Poetry and Philosophy*. Princeton: Princeton UP.
Mora, Tulio. 2009. *Los broches mayores del sonido*. Lima: Fondo Cultural Editorial Peruana.
Perloff, Marjorie. 2004. *Differentials*. Tuscaloosa: U of Alabama P.
Pimentel, Jorge. 2012. *Tromba de agosto*. Lima: Lustra Editores.
Pimentel, Jorge. 2014. *Ave Soul*. Lima: Lustra Editores.
Rosen, Stanley. 1993. *The Quarrel Between Poetry and Philosophy*. New York: Routledge.
Vallejo, César. 1922. *Trilce*. 1922. Lima: Talleres Tipográficos de la Penitenciaría.
Villacorta González, Carlos. 2017. *Poéticas de la ciudad: Lima en la poesía de los setenta*. Buenos Aires: El corregidor.

8 Turning With Heidegger Towards Poetry

Matthew Caleb Flamm

Heidegger is discussed in this chapter in order to philosophically frame the quarrel of this book. His thinking is a useful signpost, both as an historical barometer of the poetry-philosophy quarrel, and as an illustration of how one of the most influential philosophers of the twentieth century attempted to heal the inexorable rift between poetry and philosophy.[1] In this chapter I encourage readers to turn with my provocations, on loan of Heideggerian insights, to an outlook that offers a means of moving beyond the insidious oppositional position in which the Western tradition (greatly influenced by Plato) has helped place poetry and philosophy. Such a turn might place these indispensable modes of communication in a position of mutual support, enlisting them as co-creators of meaning towards understanding the human condition.

A crucial point to take away from the foregoing chapters is that poetry and philosophy stand at opposed, though by no means *necessarily* opposed, poles of language. Recalling my first chapter, considering the ancient character of Plato's fabled quarrel as it evolved in the Western tradition, the two may have always been in opposition. One explanation for this could be that these modes of language possess two distinctly seductive qualities. Poets might be said to be more easily seduced by the making power of language, while philosophers are partial to its discovering power. Perhaps too, the nature of creation itself accounts for the poetry-philosophy divide, the prodigious demands creation places on creators to derive novel insights through diverse modes of technique, rooted in something akin to what Aristotle expressed in his distinction between *poiêton* (making something) and *praktikon* (action).[2]

Whatever the correct explanation for their oppositional character, as discussed in the first chapter, the tension between the two has played out historically in the West in a manner imposing on poets a role that has (unfairly) made them harbingers of darkness, ever-posing a threat to light-bringing lovers of wisdom who have culturally enjoyed (equally unfairly) a position of privilege.

If one were to consider the contrast in terms of the use of language, one might say that poetry lovers prefer apophatic expressiveness, suggestive metaphor, ambiguity of meaning, allegory, and simile-laden imagery. Apophatic[3] meaning is derived by way of denial, or negation, a concept indicative of a particular methodological approach to divinity. Apophatic theology approaches divinity as a phenomenon beyond interpretive reach, as an absence. In its reliance upon symbolic language poetry is ideally positioned as a conduit of such divine expression. Meantime philosophy lovers are partial to cataphatic expressiveness, apodictic (indisputable) language, argument, proof, and demonstration. Cataphatic meaning[4] is derived by way of affirmation. Cataphatic theology conceives divinity in positive terms, a direct presence implied in the expression "God is love." In so far as these divergent interpretive centers are seductive preferences it is probably fruitless to look for a "solution" to their perceived opposition and in fact a better strategy is to look for harmonious unions between them. To repeat a point of my first chapter: the very perception that poetry and philosophy "oppose" one another may be at base a cultural contrivance induced by the turbulence of historical change.

Solutions to the perceived opposition between poetry and philosophy has been sought at various key points of historical time and place, most famously, as the first chapter showed, by Plato. Plato's call to protect the State from the excesses of poetry involved a reversal of the traditional attitude towards divinity, a move away from the *Iliad/Oedipus*-model in which human understanding is in need of reconciliation to (often inexplicably cruel) divine justice, to the *Odyssey*-model, which recommends a conception of the morally elect in which divinity is asked to conform with human understanding. The suppression of poetry bequeathed from Plato was a turn against negativity, against darkness, particularly as it interfaces with the concept of divine transcendence.

Historically "philosophy" in the sense established by Plato became a path-paver for today's cultural authority, science, pitting its light-shedding power to invent life-transforming material possibilities against poetry's eccentric playfulness and perceived "uselessness" in the same direction. And yet as happens in other areas of life, when something as vital as poetry is suppressed, it becomes by that very suppression notoriously powerful and inevitably leaks back into the interpretive equation.[5]

The advent in more recent history of postmodern literature and philosophy and its despairing posture towards meaning and truth has tended to encourage the view (outside of the unquestioning initiated), that poetic discourse is willfully impotent, even ridiculous. As the first chapter suggested, this fact is unfortunate if not also ironic given that it is precisely the post-modern tradition that has tried in its own way to recover the significance of the making-power of poetic discourse. This once again brings to fore the importance of historical context.

When poetry is taken seriously as a form of literature it is usually in a climate of sophisticated culture. In such climates only the "cultivated" and initiated can be said to have a "taste" for poetry. Such elitism swiftly becomes odious to the uninitiated for reasons Oscar Wilde expressed in the wonderful aphoristic preface to *The Picture of Dorian Gray* in which he diagnosed the situation of art at the end of the nineteenth century: "The nineteenth-century dislike of realism is the rage of Caliban[6] seeing his own face in a glass. The nineteenth-century dislike of romanticism is the rage of Caliban not seeing his own face in a glass."[7] The suggestion is that art at the close of the nineteenth century had reached a situation of double-bind. Resorting to realism, art was despised by its audience for its too-recognizably human, unflattering imagery (the *self*-hatred of Shakespeare's Caliban, whom, although half-human is at the same time the "only" human on an inhuman island, reviled by the fully human, conquering invaders led by Prospero); resorting to romanticism/idealism art had become despised by its audience for its too-foreign, fantastical imagery (the *alter/other-self-hatred* of Shakespeare's Caliban).[8] Extending Wilde's suggestive commentary on art at the end of the nineteenth century to this consideration of poetry: in its cultural relegation to allegedly sophisticated understanding, poetry has in modern times had to endure the double dislike of the unsophisticated. Poetry is disliked on the one hand for its vivacious "too real" imagery, yet on the other for its fancy-flights which appear to move beyond life to a point of irrelevance.

Just here is where Heidegger—mislabeled as "postmodernist"[9]—helps: "Poetry is either rejected as a frivolous mooning and vaporizing into the unknown, and a flight into dreamland, or is counted as a part of literature."[10] In this context, a 1951 lecture, Heidegger is thinking through German Romantic poet Friedrich Hölderlin's suggestion that "man dwells in poetry." The concept "dwelling" (German: *Aufenthalt, sich aufhalten*) played a piv-otal role in Heidegger's thought at least since the 1927 publication of *Being and Time*. Heidegger takes Hölderlin's "man dwells in poetry" as meaning not that poetry is some kind of realm that can be inhabited by humans, but that it is poetry which first of all permits humans to "dwell." He prefaces this fuller conclusion with acknowledgment of the conventional (mis)under-standing of "mere" poetic activity:

how can human dwelling be understood as based on the poetic? The phrase "man dwells poetically," comes indeed from a mere poet, and in fact from one who, we are told, could not cope with life.[11] It is the way of poets to shut their eyes to actuality. Instead of acting, they dream. What they make is merely imagined. The things of imagination are merely made. Making is, in Greek *poiesis*.[12]

Heidegger follows these reflections on the conventional "mere" making appearance of poetic activity by considering the "essential nature" of poetry and dwelling, which he summarizes as follows: "we are to think of what is called man's existence by way of the nature of dwelling; [and] we are to think of the nature of poetry as a letting-dwell, as a—perhaps even *the*—distinctive kind of building."[13]

The perception of poetic activity as a "mere dreaming" form of making is false: poetry *lets* humans exist, for to exist is according to Heidegger to "dwell," a concept he contrasted as early as 1927 in *Being and Time* from the sense of "dwelling in" implied in conventional relations of objective presence, as when a person stands "in" a room. Probing to a primordial sense of "dwelling," one based on the linguistic origins of the term, designating a "being in"-relation, Heidegger derived his original coinage, *Dasein*, or "there-being": "being-in designates a constitution of being of Dasein, and is an *existential*."[14] Dwelling existentially is not a relation of subject-object between-ness, where one sort of being is determined by its connection to another (as a person's awareness of her dwelling might be determined by her being "in" a room), but is rather a fundamental relation of care and familiarity, absorption in creative activity complete enough on its own to constitute a form of awareness distinct from sheer cognitive understanding.[15]

In the famous *turn* in his thinking towards poetry,[16] Heidegger preoccupied himself more exclusively with the making power of language. It would be wrong to say that Heidegger at the same time abandoned philosophy or the discovering power of language. To the contrary, it is important to observe that throughout his writings there is a consistently philosophic preoccupation: determining the basis of intelligibility or what permits humans to make sense of what there is. This preoccupation prompted Heidegger to explore the nature of interpretation (German: *Auslegung*) which he defined as "the development of understanding."[17] For Heidegger it is interpretation—acts of interpretation—that permit intelligibility, the important qualification being that such acts cannot be "looked at" in the same manner that a subject might look at and try to fathom objective external realities; interpretation is "stuck" in being in such a manner that the basis of intelligibility can only be determined, if at all, indirectly by way of implication.

Put in terms connected with the foregoing characterizations concerning the nature of poetry and philosophy, it is crucial to acknowledge the interpretive-"hermeneutic circle"[18] in which understanding becomes aware of itself. Since interpretation, the basis of intelligibility, can never stand out-side of being, there can never be a cognitively-aware *discovery* of the basis of intelligibility; acknowledgment of this, in Heidegger's view, offers the meantime possibility that an understanding of the same can be *made through language*. Enter poetry. As Simon Critchley puts it: "We are always stuck in a circle, and it is therefore a question of entering the circle in the right way and not trying to get out of it."[19] Poetic activity is a "right" manner of enter-ing into the ever moving circle of interpretation so as to permit its circularity to provoke an understanding unhindered by resistance to interpretation's circular flow, an achievement vital to artistic understanding. In contrast, non-poetic activity is the attempt to arrest for the sake of understanding an aspect of the circle of interpretation, an achievement vital to establishing empirical knowledge.

So a crucial part of why poetic language is legitimate and vital is the implicated nature of interpretation itself. Fittingly, Heidegger's inspiration on some of these points was Plato's great adversarial student, Aristotle. When in his two-volume *Analytics* Aristotle distinguished between "univer-sal, particular, or indefinite" propositions,[20] his aim was to identify the "fac-ulty of demonstration" that constitutes the carrying out of "demonstrative science." From these distinctions he derived the difference between what he called "demonstrative" and "dialectical" propositions. As Aristotle under-stood the difference, demonstrative propositions (what we would today call "scientific"), which he tended to illustrate referencing the field of geometry, prove from known premises conclusions not previously known, thereby pro-ducing knowledge. Dialectical propositions, in contrast, propositions like "not every pleasure is good," are questionable (what we would probably today term *philosophic*) assertions. Dialectical propositions depend upon persuasive techniques distinct from deductive methods of demonstrative reasoning because they rely on premises not previously known to be true.[21]

The contrast became formalized much later in the writings of Immanuel Kant (1724–1804, the great climactic figure of Modern philosophy). Kant, moved to the idea by his inspirer, classical empiricist David Hume (1711–1776), conceived dialectical reasoning as "problematic" reasoning because it establishes relations of possibility, as opposed to propositions that estab-lish relations of necessity.[22] The contrast for Kant was the same as for Aris-totle in so far as it entailed a distinction between matters of consideration given to necessary versus questionable (problematic) settlement.

Attempting to think with-and-beyond these points of inspiration, inter-ested as he was in the implicated nature of interpretation, Heidegger moved to make the distinction between "necessary" and "questioning" interpretive understanding a moot point. Critchley puts the point this way: "Interpretation already understands, and what interpretation lays out is already understood and must have been already understood."[23] The very awareness of a distinction like "necessary versus probable assertions" is a post-hoc emergence. As Heidegger's later-career *turn* indicates, poetry is the recourse; the necessary recourse of attempting to understand the nature of that which eludes emergent understanding.

Similar to the scaffolded, mechanically-perched bricklayer in relation to his building-in-progress, the builder of understanding, or builder of intelligibility (which incidentally describes the creative activity of *both* poet and philosopher), sits *within* his larger building-construct trusting to his creative-interpretive understanding the integrity of a greater understanding. Only here is the key difference: unlike the builder of material objects the intelligibility-builder can never step back from his creation to behold the "final product." The meaning he creates is ever dependent upon his (and other's) interpretive existence.

This is what makes Heidegger's thinking so complex for readers, and what leads so many to wrongly consider his thought to be sheer obscurantism ("postmodern" in the bad sense). "Too many readers of Heidegger see being as some kind of rabbit in a hat. There is no rabbit. The point is to learn to see the hat without wanting the rabbit";[24] to see, in other words, the magic of building-in-creation without having to see the finished product. From Heidegger's point of view, the *building* that poetic interpretation undertakes gets confused with the kind of building undertaken in material contexts because of a conceit humans have about language and understanding:

> How far man is from being at home in his own essence is revealed by his opinion of himself as he who invented and could have invented language and understanding, building and poetry. How could man ever have invented the power which pervades him, which alone enables him to be a man?[25]

Poetic creative activity is a power pervading the human situation, enabling beings like us to be human in the first place.

An important recursive point occurs here: Plato fought for philosophy against poetry because he thought the good of society was at stake, a concern requiring searchlight, as opposed to footlight intelligence. For Plato poetry, in its ability to excite unsavory passions, has the potential of undermining one's ability to control oneself intelligently:

> Poetry has the same effect on us when it represents sex and anger, and the other desires and feelings of pleasure and pain which accompany all our actions. It waters them when they ought to be left to wither,

and makes them control us when we ought, in the interests of our own greater welfare and happiness, to control them.[26]

The searchlight intelligence of philosophic creation—its discovery-seeking nature—was for Plato the best means to achieve social order and control.

For Heidegger such considerations were of derivative importance and questions of ontology and intelligibility (how things come into awareness in the first place) were of primary importance.[27] He understood the basis of intelligibility to be positioned primordially beyond reach of the sort of understanding found in the social and empirical sciences. His topical turn to poetry came from a long-held conviction as to the ontological status of interpretive expression. Indeed for Heidegger the human situation, *Dasein* ("there-being," imperfectly translated as "being-in-the-world") is something about which humans initially become aware in a mode of "average understanding," which entails a relation "in which we are always already involved."[28]

Heidegger helps one see how historically philosophers, given to extremes, have misconceived interpretation. Either they have coveted and courted the proverbial "view from nowhere"[29] according to which the only valuable ideas are ones derived from detached, impersonal, aspiringly objective perspectives, or they have sought the Hegelian "view from everywhere," the extreme of subjectivism according to which all of reality is the absolute unfolding of the mind of God. From Heidegger's point of view there is no more a "view from nowhere" than there is a Hegelian "view from everywhere." All views are for Heidegger vitally *some*-where,[30] and this opens the need to acknowledge the *footlight* nature of interpretive understanding, an acknowledgment for which there is arguably no better mode than poetry.

If temporality, as Heidegger contends—no less in the conjunct of the title of his most famous book—is ontologically determinative towards understanding the human situation, the human relation to language is decisive as a means of assessing the intelligibility of experience and existence. As already indicated, poetry is a particular relation to language. So is philosophy. Their tendency to quarrel thus has to do with the nature of language. The conventional, or default distinction between poetic and non-poetic language is the poetry-prose dichotomy. Heidegger helps one see that how this dichotomy is false, erasing recognition of what was earlier identified as the existential "dwelling" phenomenon of poetic language. He observes that the tendency to see poetic and non-poetic discourse as delivered in language through modes of *poetry* versus *prose* comes from a narrowing of the conception of language to "expression." Conceiving language merely as "expression" is to see *utterance* as language, but neither "utterance, let alone expression, [should be conceived as] the decisive element of human speech."[31] Leaving open what precisely *is* the decisive element of human speech, Heidegger identifies the missing elements of the language-as-expression conception to be listening and acceptance: "Mortals speak insofar as they listen . . . [the] speaking that listens and accepts is responding."[32]

Poetry is, yes, an "expression," but a very special form of one it is repressive to restrict to that characterization. Poetry is a form of expression that is *listening* and *accepting* of a world and living situation that is the world's creaturely ground; it is an openness to the "bidding of the world."[33] In contrast so-identified "prose" is a misleading placeholder-name for *un*-poetic expression:

> The opposite of what is purely spoken, the opposite of the poem, is not prose. Pure prose is never "prosaic." It is as poetic and hence as rare as poetry.[34]

The very idea that writing and kindred discourse is categorically distinct from poetry misconceives interpretation, which, in order to include listening, must according to Heidegger have already exercised expressive restraint in what he calls a "peal of stillness."[35] This is Heidegger's understanding of poetic insight. It involves listening restraint. To the extent that there is something akin to what Heidegger terms "pure prose" it involves something else, something not opposed to listening restraint—indeed, it must, by his same conception involve the same—but delivered in an expressive mode different enough from poetry to merit the conventional distinction between the two. Prose, conventionally defined as a "natural" or "ordinary" flow of speech and writing, is fluid and flowing precisely when it is poetic.

An excellent reference point for this that also serves as an apt conclusion to the foregoing comes from an author whom, because of his unique poetic genius,[36] is ideally positioned to provide insight. The reference comes from a 1940s lecture-essay, "The Figure of the Youth as Virile Poet," by Wallace Stevens. Stevens begins the piece invoking iconoclastic vitalist philosopher Henri Bergson. Stevens quotes a perspective offered by philosopher William James who, upon completing Bergson's *Creative Evolution*, wrote to its author: "I found [in reading *Creative Evolution*] the same after-taste remaining as after finishing *Madame Bovary*, such a flavor of persistent euphony."[37] James's sentiment together with some cited skeptical remarks about philosophy moves Stevens to endorse the idea that poetry offers an "unofficial view of being." He elaborates:

> To define poetry as an unofficial view of being places it in contrast with philosophy and at the same time establishes the relationship between the two. . . . We must conceive of poetry as at least the equal of

philosophy. If truth is the object of both and if any considerable number of people feel very skeptical of all philosophers, then, to be brief about it, a still more considerable number of people must feel very skeptical of all poets.[38]

Stevens proceeds from these reflections to note the different manners in which philosophic versus poetic ideas find their justification. One is skeptical of philosophic ideas, he observes, because they fail to satisfy reason, whereas skepticism in regard to poetic ideas occurs because they fail to satisfy the imagination. A key further difference between the two (and this is a point Stevens makes though not in this exact way) is that although they may possess imaginative (poetic) elements, philosophic ideas need not do so and in fact are valued independently of such; evaluating a philosophic idea one need only point to the sound or unsound *reason* that is its ground in order to pronounce it legitimate or objectionable. If in addition to being rationally valued a philosophic idea also has imaginative, poetic elements, this will be a kind of unnecessary, if also pleasant, unexpected bonus. By contrast, the key thing about the evaluation of a poetic idea is that "If an imaginative idea does not satisfy the imagination, our expectation of it is not fulfilled." The evaluative ground of a poetic idea *is* in other words its imaginative fulfillment and poetry thus has no need, as in the case of philosophy, for a mediatory reasoning sanction.

When, as is presumably rare, a poetic idea happens also to have rational sanction—Stevens offers by way of illustration an idea of God that is expressed to "establish a divine beginning and end for us which, at the moment, the reason, singly, at best proposes and on which, at the moment, the imagination, singly, merely meditates"—this too is a happy, if unnecessary, achievement. But what an achievement it is compared to the philosophic one! Such an achievement, Stevens argues, does not place the poet in the position of philosopher, "On the contrary, if the end of the philosopher is despair, the end of the poet is fulfillment, since the poet finds a sanction for life in poetry that satisfies the imagination." If a philosopher can be said to sanction reason, the poet sanctions life, a sanction outside of which no reason can satisfy. These provocations map perfectly on to Heidegger's *dwelling* conception of poetry. Poetry is vital—arguably more vital than philosophy—in its offering a sanction for life.

There is a saying (once paraphrased to me by a former professor) that William James wrote philosophy like literature, while his famous literary brother Henry wrote literature like philosophy. Philosophers such as Emerson, Santayana, and Nietzsche have been ridiculed on the grounds of their "poetic" and "literary" modes of presentation. The odd expectation that philosophy (and in some quarters, literature) shed its "adorning" language has a fairly recent historical basis, and the profession of philosophy in modern times is a poignant marker. Philosophy in the first half of the twentieth century was thoroughly afflicted by a disciplinary schism that persists to this day, eventuating in the so-called Continental and analytic philosophic divide: between those privileging literature as an interpretive inspiration and those privileging mathematical logic and the empirical sciences. Poets and philosophers may have always quarreled but historically recent developments within the profession reveal a deeper quarrel within philosophy itself.[39]

In effect, Heidegger asks in his later career, why cannot the philosopher rise to the level of the poet? Turning to poetry, in a sense striving to encourage a turn *in* philosophy, Heidegger identifies the "thinker" as capable of rising to the level of the poet, and of rescuing the philosopher from his philosophic deafness: "We may know something about the relations between philosophy and poetry, but we know nothing of the dialogue between poet and thinker, who 'dwell near to one another on mountains farthest apart.'"[40] The near-yet-far relation between poet and thinker might be reestablished, Heidegger suggests, if the philosopher comes once again to be capable of "uttering being":

> Out of long-guarded speechlessness and the careful clarification of the field thus cleared, comes the utterance of the thinker. Of like origin is the naming of the poet . . . since poetry and thinking are most purely alike in their care of the word, the two things are at the same time at opposite poles in their essence. The thinker utters Being. The poet names what is holy.[41]

Notes

1. Clarification should be provided about the "turning" of my chapter title. The question of the meaning of *die Kehr* or "the turning" as understood in association with Heidegger's writings is a matter of immensely complex discussion in scholarship, and while it is beyond dispute that he became increasingly preoccupied with poetry, the philosophic "turning" of Heidegger's thought after the 1927 publication of *Being and Time* involves much more than an increased preoccupation with poetry. Heidegger's thought and writings as a whole never stopped "turning" as he was in a continual mode of "responding." He explains this in a June 1950 letter to a young student reflecting on the lack of any singular "directive" in his work: "thinking of Being is a highly errant and in addition a very destitute matter. Thinking is perhaps, after all, an unavoidable path, which refuses to be a path of salvation and brings no new wisdom. . . . Everything depends on the step back, fraught with error, into the thoughtful reflection that attends the turnabout of the oblivion of Being, the turnabout that

is prefigured in the destiny of Being. The step back from the representational thinking of metaphysics does not reject such thinking, but opens the distant to the appeal of the trueness of Being in which the responding always takes place." Martin Heidegger. *Poetry, Language, Thought.* Translated by Albert Hofstadter. Harper & Row Publishers, 1971: end-book letter. Examples of rich scholarly considerations of the meaning of *die Kehr* in Heidegger's career include: Kelly Edward Mink. "Heidegger: Ontology, Metontology, and the Turn" (dissertation available via the Loyola University Chicago E-commons: https://ecommons. luc.edu/cgi/viewcontent.cgi?article=3560&context=luc_diss); Laurence Hemming. "Speaking out of Turn: Martin Heidegger and die Kehre." *International Journal of Philosophical Studies*, 6(3), October 1998: 393–423; *Heidegger Toward the Turn: Essays on the Work of the 1930's.* James Risser. SUNY Series in Contemporary Continental Philosophy, eBook, 1999. Heidegger discusses "The Turning" in a lecture of 1949 titled "Insight."

2. In the *Nicomachean Ethics* Aristotle distinguishes between the disposition (hexis) particular to making and the disposition tied to acting. For Aristotle, the difference between making something (*poiêton*) and activity (*praktikon*) is a difference between forms of creation whose end is an activity-distinct product (an art work, for example), and forms of creation that are ends-in-themselves, self-justifying forms of activity aimed at discovery.

3. Greek: *apophatikos* "negative," *apophasis* "denial."

4. Greek *kataphatikos* "affirmative," *kataphasis* "affirmation."

5. At various key moments of historical time after Plato's attacks upon it poetry achieved a reputation that, for example, in Dante's Renaissance Italy, in the Modern-epoch-making works of Shakespeare, and later in the nineteenth century novel, it only seems to have had its "negative-bringing" stock raised as possessing a special power to make meaning.

6. Caliban, son of Sycorax, a witch, is a central character in Shakespeare's *The Tempest.* Enslaved by Prospero, Caliban is a conflicted character of contradictions.

7. Oscar Wilde. "The Picture of Dorian Gray." *The Portable Oscar Wilde.* Edited by Richard Aldington and Stanley Weintraub. Penguin Books, 1981: 138.

8. Wilde himself can be said to have brilliantly split the difference between realism and romanticism by embracing fairy tale, gothic, and hyper-fantastic modes of presentation, a literary move that, exemplified in *Dorian Gray*, achieves through modes of the fantastic an uncanny sensation of reality. Wilde's is a kind of innovative literary method of symbolism or allegory. Many brilliant twentieth-century literary figures made similar moves to evade the bypass. To name two on the American side, in the North American tradition Sherwood Anderson's grotesque realism, and in the South American tradition Gabriel García Márquez's magical realism are examples of literary modes resolving the realism-romanticism stalemate.

9. The many examples of characteristic "postmodernists" inspired by elements of Heidegger's work such as Derrida notwithstanding. Maybe "anti-modernist" fits, but Heidegger's multifaceted, comprehensive critique of the Western tradition as a whole makes the characterization "postmodernist" at best highly selective and begs controversial qualification.

10. Martin Heidegger. ". . . Poetically Man Dwells . . ." *Poetry, Language, Thought.* Translated by Albert Hofstadter. Harper & Row Publishers, 1971: 213.

11. In the 1790s Hölderlin (1770–1843) was diagnosed as schizophrenic and had various stays in clinics.

12. Martin Heidegger. "... Poetically Man Dwells ..." *Poetry, Language, Thought.* Translated by Albert Hofstadter. Harper & Row Publishers, 1971: 214.

13. Ibid., 215.

14. *BT,* § 12, 54 (Stambaugh).

15. A primordial relation of being-in-the-world more fundamental than subject-object relations of presence. Heidegger speaks of "thinking" and "building" in synonymy with this dwelling relation. His close association of "Building Dwelling Thinking" is illustrated in a same-titled lecture delivered in 1951 ("*Bauen Wohnen Denken*"): the absence of hyphenation or commas indicates his aim to cross-identify these concepts.

16. Reminding here of the interpretive license taken in this characterization as suggested in the opening and in note 2.

17. BT, § 32, pg. 132 (Stambaugh).

18. Hermeneutics is the "art of interpretation." The term "hermeneutics" comes from the name of the messenger or "interpreter" of the Greek Gods, Hermes, which gave rise to the Greek word *hermēneuein* ("to interpret") and *hermēneutike* (*technē*). The "hermeneutic circle" is an unending circle of interpretation whereby one is interpretively locked, as it were, in an ever-flowing cycle; how one interprets and understands one's experiences influences the way one experiences things, which influences how one interprets one's experiences, and so on in an unending circle. Although he is not himself the first to identify the hermeneutic circle, German theologian Friedrich Schleiermacher (1768–1834) is credited with having been an originator of the concept and inspirer of Heidegger's development of the notion.

19. Simon Critchley. "What is the Meaning of the Meaning of Being?" *After Heidegger?* Edited by Gregory Fried and Richard Polt. Rowman & Littlefield, 2018: 235.

20. Aristotle. *Prior Analytics,* 24a 17.

21. For Aristotle demonstrative and dialectical arguers differ in whether the premise-poser is "asking" something: in the former demonstrative assertion case the poser is "not asking for" her premise, but "laying it down" (24a 24); the latter, questionable assertion "depends on the adversary's choice between two contradictories."

22. The infamous "synthetic-analytic" distinction inaugurated by Kant on inspiration from his teacher Hume: synthetic propositions are constructed, world-dependent claims, analytic propositions are self-evidently meaningful: "All crows are black" (synthetic, contingent), "A bachelor is an unmarried male" (analytic, definitional).

23. Simon Critchley. "What is the Meaning of the Meaning of Being?" *After Heidegger?* Edited by Gregory Fried and Richard Polt. Rowman & Littlefield, 2018: 234.

24. Ibid., 234.

25. Martin Heidegger. *An Introduction to Metaphysics.* Translated by Ralph Manheim. Yale University Press, 1959: 156.

26. *Republic,* 606d.

27. Undoubtedly there is a connection between this aspect of Heidegger's thought and his troubling connections with Nazism. In 1933, having been appointed Rector of the University of Freiburg, Heidegger became a member of the Nazi party and remained a member through to the end of the war (and of the Nazi party). To the end of his life he remained virtually silent, at best evasive, about

the Holocaust and his Nazi membership, and in recent years his controversial "Black Notebooks"—personally scribed reflections that have since 2014 been released in installments to the public—contain anti-Semitic elements. Several books and much scholarship has been produced indicting Heidegger on these facts, the most indicting among them either making a case for a connection between his philosophic project and anti-Semitism, or otherwise arguing that his thought is friendly to fascist political strategies.

28. BT, § 1 chapter 2: 8 (Stambaugh).
29. See Thomas Nagel. *The View from Nowhere*. Oxford University Press, 1986.
30. The some-where view Heidegger takes to be indicative of interpretations is a result of his analysis of the ontologically temporal structure of the interpretive-human situation, of what he terms *Dasein*: "The meaning of the being of that being we call Da-sein proves to be temporality [*Zeitlichkeit*]." BT, § 5, 17.
31. Martin Heidegger. "Language." *Poetry, Language, Thought*. Translated by Albert Hofstadter. Harper & Row Publishers, 1971: 209.
32. Ibid.
33. Ibid., 206.
34. Ibid., 208.
35. Ibid., 209.
36. Incidentally educated (while at Harvard) and significantly influenced by philosopher-poet George Santayana.
37. Wallace Stevens. "The Figure of the Youth as a Virile Poet." *The Necessary Angel: Essays on Reality and the Imagination*. Alfred A. Knopf, 1951: 40.
38. Ibid., 41–42, for this quote and all further Stevens' quotes.
39. According to Richard Rorty, Heidegger's poet possesses "the ability to hear, the ability to have a sense of the contingency of [his] words and practices, and thus of the possibility of alternatives to them." Rorty alleges that in contrast philosophers lack this hearing ability and believe "that what matters is literal truth . . . not metaphors." He goes so far as to claim that "there is a prima facie opposition between the dreams of literature and the dreams of philosophy." Richard Rorty. "Heidegger, Contingency, and Pragmatism." *Essays on Heidegger and Others*. Cambridge University Press, 1991: 34, 48, 89.
40. Heidegger, Marin. "What is Metaphysics?" *Existence and Being*. Introduction and analysis by Werner Brock. Gateway Edition, Henry Regnery Co., 1968: 360.
41. Ibid., 360.

References

Aristotle. *Nicomachean Ethics*. Translation, Glossary, and Introductory Essay by Joe Sachs. Focus Publishing, 2002.

———. "Prior and Posterior Analytics." *The Basic Works of Aristotle*. Edited and with an Introduction by Richard McKeon. Random House, 1941: 65–186.

Critchley, Simon. "What is the Meaning of the Meaning of Being?" *After Heidegger*? Edited by Gregory Fried and Richard Polt. New York: Rowman & Littlefield, 2018.

Heidegger, Martin. *Being and Time*. Translated by Joan Stambaugh. SUNY Press, 1996.

————. *Poetry, Language, Thought*. Translated by Albert Hofstadter. Harper & Row, Publishers, 1971 "What is Metaphysics?" in *Existence and Being*. Introduction and analysis by Werner Brock. Gateway Edition, Henry Regnery Co., 1968.

Hemming, Laurence. "Speaking Out of Turn: Martin Heidegger and die Kehre." *International Journal of Philosophical Studies*, 6(3), October 1998: 393–423.

Mink, Kelly Edward. "Heidegger: Ontology, Metontology, and the Turn." Dissertation via the Loyola University Chicago E-commons: https://ecommons.luc.edu/cgi/viewcontent.cgi?article=3560&context=luc_diss

Nagel, Thomas. *The View from Nowhere*. Oxford Univerity Press, 1986.

Risser, James. *Heidegger Toward the Turn: Essays on the Work of the 1930's*. James Risser. SUNY Press, 1999.

Rorty, Richard. "Heidegger, Contingency, and Pragmatism." *Essays on Heidegger and Others*. Cambridge University Press, 1991.

Stevens, Wallace. "The Figure of the Youth as a Virile Poet." *The Necessary Angel: Essays on Reality and the Imagination*. Alfred A. Knopf, 1951.

Wilde, Oscar. *The Picture of Dorian Gray*. Edited by Richard Aldington and Stanley Weintraub. Penguin Books, 1981.

Coda

For the four of us, the essays in this book are triangulated among three places: the library, the classroom, and the living room.

We begin with the library because this is where our common readings of several works cited here, for example, Stanley Rosen, sent us on a regular basis. We also returned to books we had not read carefully in decades, such as the work of Sir Thomas More or Heidegger, or to encounter new intellectual figures whose work was unfamiliar before reading our colleague's essays, such as Hermann Broch or Thomas Gould's work on Plato. There is a famous Robert Duncan poem titled "Often I am permitted to return to a field" in which he describes that field, that place of knowing deeply, as a "place of first permission." We equate that to the everlasting status of being a student, a privilege which those of who are fortunate enough to work in academia enjoy. To be thorough, the bars where we sometimes met to discuss Rosen were probably just as important, but those are essays for another book.

The classroom we are thinking of is mainly the one in which we teach or take 100- or 200-level courses. Courses like first-year seminar, which all of us have had the pleasure of teaching at Rockford University and Bard College, or other courses where the texts were translated into English from Spanish, Latin, Greek, German, and French and the syllabi were designed for non-majors. This is the classroom where the clichéd rubber meets the road and we ask and, at least to some extent, answer an essential question with our students: do these texts matter? Do they speak to our reality and help us cope with it, resist it, and reimagine it? This is a classroom of sudden and meaningful discoveries, where a student might let out a gasp when what had before seemed to be a hermetic classic all of a sudden makes sense, where we can find our footing to argue with the authors we have been trained to read and begin to question why we have been trained to read them in the first place. A consensus of dissent and affirmation.

We mention the living room because this is where the shock of the political often hits us hardest. We see the notification on the smartphone that makes us wonder what is the latest bit of news that will make us even more worried. We might ignore it for a bit, but will eventually look at it and wonder what words and ideas, when we get back to the classroom, we can still use, what we can rescue from this onslaught of misinformation, willful ignorance, and hatred that is spreading in the world the four of us inhabit. Before the 2016 election we thought, or at least hoped, that the comments about the grabbing of women or the labeling of Mexicans as rapists and murderers would clearly disqualify anyone who would utter them from serving in political office. After the election, the words became actions, with the proposed Muslim ban, the attempted border wall, and the emboldening of ICE agents who seem to act with increasing impunity. The continued dismissal of the truth (largest turnout ever for an inauguration, an African nation named "Nambia," a "perfect phone call," and so on) made our heads spin.

As outrageous as it all was and seems still to be (as we prepare this manuscript for submission in March 2020, administration officials are calling the coronavirus outbreak a "hoax"), we had templates for thinking about the crisis of language and thought we were, and still are, living through. We reached for texts that helped us to consider abstractly the "now" through the lens of a "then." We have thought about noble lies, the distrust of language, upside down historical realities, and the ways in which the arts, in the service of the political, have sought to manipulate others in different times and places. Moving through distinct periods of time and sweeping geographies, the essays then also move through all three intimate spaces, library, classroom, and living room, and in so doing unite, to some degree, the discourse of each without diminishing any one of them.

We are far from alone in this task. None other than Lin-Manuel Miranda in an article in *The Atlantic* (December 2019 print edition) reminds us that "All art is political" because "[a]rt lives in the world." Nato Thompson's recent book *Culture as Weapon* reminds us that manipulating emotions through popular culture and social media "has become inseparable from power" (2018, x). Five of the authors and figures studied in this book experienced the consequences of historical power firsthand: Socrates, executed via hemlock in 399 BCE; Boethius, condemned and executed probably in 526; Thomas More, beheaded in 1535; Sir Philip Sidney, died of an injury received fighting the Spanish for the Protestant cause in 1586; and Broch, imprisoned in 1938 and thereafter a refugee from Nazi Europe along with many artists and scholars. The representations of La Malinche occur against the backdrop of a brutal process of colonization. In Peru, Hora Zero existed in the context of a military junta that had little tolerance for dissent. The philosophies discussed here—Plato, Aristotle, Heidegger, Derrida, Rorty, and others—are engaged across a huge space of time in the same question: what is true and how do we know? And in exploring that question, the moderns return to the ancients, to learn, discard, revise. Writers as diverse as Broch and Pimentel engaged in radical revision of received traditions, as did the icons of tradition such as Shakespeare and Vergil on the traditions they inherited.

The bad news is that right now the issue of truth is contested as never before in our lifetimes. The good news is that our training as scholars and our vocations as teachers equip us and compel us to engage in the contest and, we hope, enlarge our own capacity to learn and share our exploration with others. The friendship among us four has been the icing on the academic cake!

Reference

Thompson, Nato. 2018. *Culture as Weapon: The Art of Influence in Everyday Life*. Melville House paperback.

Index

Printed in the United States
by Baker & Taylor Publisher Services